The
Enlightened
Despots

Berkshire Studies

in European History

Under the editorship of
Richard A. Newhall and Sidney R. Packard

THE CRUSADES, Revised Edition
Richard A. Newhall, *Emeritus, Williams College*

THE RENAISSANCE
Wallace K. Ferguson, *Western Ontario University*

THE REFORMATION, Third Edition
George L. Mosse, *University of Wisconsin*

THE AGE OF LOUIS XIV
Laurence B. Packard, *late of Amherst College*

THE ENLIGHTENED DESPOTS, Second Edition
Geoffrey Bruun

THE RISE OF BRANDENBURG-PRUSSIA TO 1786,
Revised Edition
Sidney B. Fay, *Emeritus, Harvard University*
Revised by Klaus Epstein, *Brown University*

THE FRENCH REVOLUTION
Leo Gershoy, *New York University*

THE AGE OF METTERNICH, 1814–1848,
Revised Edition
Arthur J. May, *University of Rochester*

IMPERIAL RUSSIA
Michael Karpovich, *late of Harvard University*

THE BALKANS, 1815–1914
L. S. Stavrianos, *Northwestern University*

THE RISE OF MODERN COMMUNISM
Revised Edition
Massimo Salvadori, *Smith College*

The
Enlightened
Despots

SECOND EDITION

by

Geoffrey Bruun

HOLT, RINEHART and WINSTON
New York   Chicago   San Francisco   Toronto   London

The illustrations on the cover are portraits of
Frederick II, Catharine II, and Joseph II.
(The Granger Collection)

24977

Preface

The faiths and fears of an earlier generation, the passions and the poses that swayed people now dead, can never be revived "in living color." But it *is* possible to retrace the pattern of their thinking and to be stirred from afar by the intensity of their aspirations. This brief study is intended primarily to convey an impression of the eighteenth-century temper, of the eighteenth-century frame of mind and mood. That incandescent mood, intense, sanguine, and sometimes naive, is the clue to the age of enlightenment. Without such a clue, without compassion for the dream of a perfected world which dazzled that hopeful age, the romantic revolt, the French Revolution, and the epic of Napoleon would remain unmotivated pageants lacking the pulse of life.

The preparation of a second edition of *The Enlightened Despots* has afforded me the happy opportunity to recast and expand many of the original passages, to attach a short introduction, and to bring the bibliographical note up to date. I am most grateful to the publishers for the critical suggestions they obtained from three specialists in the field, suggestions which I have incorporated, so far as I was able, to the marked benefit of the book. There is, regrettably, too little space to list here the friends and colleagues whose encouragement lightened my labor. Still less would it be possible to name the many students who, by their quick interest and lively response, have provided me over the years with the teacher's strongest incentive and truest reward. To all of them my greeting and my gratitude.

G. B.

October 1966

Contents

Introduction:
The Evolution of Law
and Government

• *The Origins of Kingship* In ancient times people worshiped their kings as gods, or if they did not regard them as actual divinities, they believed them to be descendants of the gods who could still communicate with those awesome beings. The earliest kings were also priests and magicians whose incantations were intended to appease and win the favor of the mysterious deities that controlled the world. As kingdoms expanded into empires, the power and dignity of the rulers increased. The Pharaohs of Egypt became god-kings who after death were said to live forever in the company of their fellow immortals. In the early Babylonian cities the kings were frequently pictured conversing with the gods, and receiving from them a code of laws by which to govern their subjects. The Bible tells how "the Lord spake unto Moses, face to face, as a man speaketh unto his friend," and how Moses copied onto tablets of stone the Ten Commandments the Lord revealed to him for the guidance of the Israelites.

Where laws come from, how they are made, and who is to interpret and enforce them are profound questions that men· have debated for thousands of years. The answers they have found may be listed under two main classifications: (1) the argument that the authority of the laws comes from above, from a supernatural source, or (2) the argument that the authority of the laws comes from the people and that "govern-

1

ments derive their just powers from the consent of the governed."

In most ancient kingdoms and empires the laws were accepted as coming from above: the people regarded them as divine commands. The gods, it was believed, had revealed a code of law to the king, to inspired prophets, or to the priests and oracles in the temples. Until recent times a large majority of the world's people accepted this view. Egyptian pharaohs, Babylonian kings, Roman, Byzantine, and Chinese emperors, Moslem caliphs, Aztec and Inca rulers—all were either worshiped as divinities or honored as the spokesmen, the living representatives, of the celestial powers. The laws issued by these rulers were believed to carry a supernatural authority, to be edicts ordained and enforced to satisfy the inscrutable will of the gods. To criticize, to defy such edicts was not only civil disobedience, but religious heresy and blasphemy.

• *Athenian Democracy* Yet even in the ancient world there were independent-minded peoples who dared to throw off the rule of kings and make their own laws. By the fifth century B.C. several Greek cities had become republics, ruled by elected magistrates and councils. Athens, the most famous of the Greek city-states, took the lead in defying the Persians when the "Great King" who ruled the Persian empire attempted to conquer Greece. The struggle that followed saw the Persian forces defeated on land and sea. To the Athenians, their success appeared proof that free men who fought voluntarily were clearly superior to the slavish subjects of an absolute monarch who fought at his command.

The Greeks were a highly gifted people, and Greek philosophers pondered deeply on problems of government. The most famous of these philosophers were Socrates (?469–399 B.C.) Plato (427-347 B.C.), and Aristotle (384-322 B.C.). All of them agreed that the ideal city would be one in which the citizens felt as much concern for public affairs as for their own private interests. This ideal was most nearly realized in Athens. Any male Athenian citizen might be chosen by lot to serve on the governing council or as a member of the court that tried lawbreakers. Consequently, it was essential for all male citizens to have some knowledge of law and politics. Questions to be decided were first clarified by rational analysis. Free discussions permitted each citizen to express his opinion and learn what his neighbors thought. When a question came before the council and a majority of the council agreed on a decision, all male citizens could feel that they had had some share, some responsibility, in shaping that decision. Pericles, who led the Athenians in the years of their greatest glory, boasted with reason that in Athens "the administration is in the hands of the many and not of the few."

Yet the Greeks also recognized that the people might sometimes make unwise choices, that democracy could degenerate into mob rule. Some of their thinkers came to feel that government by one farsighted and intelligent man—a legislator of genius—was sounder and safer than control by a number of ordinary citizens. To this argument others replied that the best when corrupted becomes the worst. However beneficial it might be to live under a powerful but benevolent ruler, a philosopher-king, there could be no guarantee that such a ruler might not change with time and become a tyrant. Tyranny, to the Greeks, appeared to be the worst of all possible governments. For a tyrant might trample on law and custom, enslave the people to serve his own ambition, and silence those who opposed him by crushing them with unlawful force.

Thus in politics, as in many other fields, the Greeks explored alternatives and expressed judgments that still remain important and meaningful today. Greek thinkers described the ideal form of government as a government that all the citizens support, a government that rests on reason instead of force, on persuasion instead of coercion. But not even the Athenians found a way to obtain and preserve this ideal form of government. After the brief and brilliant age of Pericles, Athens went down to defeat in the terrible Peloponnesian War (431-404 B.C.). In the century that followed, the Greek cities fought and weakened one another until they were forced into submission by Philip of Macedon.

Philip's famous son, Alexander the Great, extended his conquests from the Mediterranean Sea to the Indus Valley. Greek learning and Greek culture spread rapidly until it influenced most of the ancient world. But the city-states like Athens, which had been the cradles of that unique culture, were absorbed into the large polyglot empires that became dominant in the third and second centuries B.C. The generals who carved up Alexander's conquests after his early death (323 B.C.) did not establish city-states or democratic republics. They set up monarchies, and their successors claimed to rule by divine authority. The brief Greek attempt to establish governments in which the authority came from the people had failed.

● *Roman Law* By the first century B.C. the peoples living around the Mediterranean Sea had been drawn into closer contact through the expansion of Roman power. The Romans were less brilliant and imaginative than the Greeks but they surpassed them as administrators and lawgivers.

Rome, in the last five centuries B.C., evolved from a small city-state into the capital of a vast empire. Like the Athenians, Roman jurists attached great importance to the concept of natural law, an idea previously suggested by Greek philosophers. They came to the conclusion that "Nature has established rational principles for all that is," and that "Nothing is evil that is in accordance with Nature." Assuming this to be so, it followed logically that men ought to live by the natural rules, the rational principles that nature had established for them. Using right reason, thoughtful legislators should be able to frame law codes that would be in harmony with natural law. The great Roman jurist and orator, Marcus Tullius Cicero (106–43 B. C.), expressed this ideal clearly and forcibly. "True law," he wrote, "is right reason in agreement with nature."

If nature had indeed provided rational rules to guide men in their daily life, such rules should hold true for all men because all were equally children of nature. Yet different peoples had different customs, and activities freely permitted in one country were sometimes forbidden in another. Nevertheless, behind all the varieties, the divergencies of local custom, Roman jurists believed they could discern some general principles that all peoples accepted as right and just. These universal principles they sought to incorporate in a body of legislation known as the law of peoples or nations (*jus gentium*).

Roman law, finally systematized and codified in the reign of the Byzantine emperor Justinian (A. D. 527–565), exerted a profound influence on later European concepts of government and legislation. But with the collapse of the Roman Empire in the West, European civilization suffered a setback, a reversal, that lasted for centuries.

• *Medieval Society*   The collapse of the Roman Empire in western Europe, the decline of trade, of city life, and of urban culture, plunged Europe into a state of semibarbarism. The population shrank, roads and bridges fell into disrepair, and people became dependent on the food they could raise from the land they tilled. Five centuries passed before the Europeans arrested the decline. By approximately A. D. 1000 the population began to increase again. Recovery was due in part to the rise of a feudal fighting caste that could defend Europe against destructive invasions similar to those of the Huns, Northmen, and Moslems in the preceding centuries.

During the early Middle Ages, when transport and communication broke down, most Europeans found themselves restricted to isolated hamlets. Miles of swamp or forest might separate them from the next village. In this scattered and disorganized society, the institution that did most to preserve culture and unity was the Roman Catholic Church. The Church, which had grown up within the Roman Empire, survived when the western half of the Empire collapsed. The popes at Rome took over some of the titles and responsibilities of the former emperors, and churchmen kept the Latin language alive. The Church ritual and Church services gave all Catholics a common bond and a common heritage of faith. Missionaries and monks helped to spread Christ's kingdom (Christendom) into Germany, Poland, Hungary, and Scandinavia—regions the Roman armies had never conquered.

Another institution that helped to shape medieval society was feudalism. The feudal system had no orderly form or systematic organization. Rather, it was a widespread but more or less haphazard mode of landholding, under which a vassal was given a landed estate (a fief) and paid homage to a superior in return for it. To this superior the vassal owed loyalty and military service. From the ninth to the fifteenth century the hierarchy of hereditary feudal landholders, the feudal nobility, remained one of the two privileged groups in European society, the other privileged group being the clergy. By the sixteenth century the revival of towns and trade and the growing power of national monarchs had begun to undermine the power and importance of both of these privileged groups, but the nobles and the clergy clung tenaciously to their incomes and their privileges.

Land and the produce of the land were the chief forms of wealth in the Middle Ages. But land required workers to tend the herds and cultivate the grainfields, orchards, and vineyards. This helps to explain a second medieval institution, the manorial system. During the drastic and lawless centuries that followed the collapse of the Roman Empire in the West, peasants and herdsmen found it essential to win the good will of some local leader who could protect them. Country villages, where the dwellers could raise their own food, survived while towns decayed. Thousands of small hamlets became self-sufficient units known as manors, and a "lord of the manor" administered and protected each tiny domain. In return, his peasants cultivated his fields for him two or three days a week and worked on their own small plots the rest of the time. Most of these peasants became serfs, hereditary bondsmen, who owed work and other obligations to the lord of the manor and could not leave the land without his consent.

The term "feudalism" is often used loosely to include manorialism. It is more accurate, however, to recognize these institutions as related but separate systems, and to speak of the feudal and manorial institutions or the feudal-manorial system.

• *The Royal Prerogative* By the close of the Middle Ages the threefold division of society into clergy, nobles, and commoners had ceased to be just or realistic. As trade revived and towns became important once more, new groups arose that did not fit into the three-class pattern of medieval society. The confusion and multiplicity of feudal customs offended the townsmen and obstructed commerce. Merchants wanted more uniform laws and tariffs, a single system of coinage, and protection for themselves and their goods when they traveled. So long as each jealous feudal noble remained the master in his petty domain, these benefits could not easily be won.

In most European countries during the later Middle Ages, hereditary kings labored to impose their authority on their turbulent feudal nobles. Merchants and businessmen saw in the struggling monarchs the protectors they needed. With the aid of money from the townsmen, kings hired mercenary troops to help them subdue rebellious barons. Larger and larger areas became subject to the king's doom (law), became, that is, part of a *kingdom* subject to the royal jurisdiction. Permanent armed forces took form to guard the monarch (the King's Army). A standard monetary system emerged (the King's Coinage). Main roads came under royal protection (the King's Highway). An increasing number of legal decisions passed from feudal courts to the royal tribunals (the King's Justice).

By the sixteenth century the monarchs who ruled the centralized territorial states of Europe had begun to claim absolute power. Three factors in particular helped to explain the rise of royal absolutism at the close of the Middle Ages. First, the revival of towns and trade, as already noted, enriched the townsmen, the burgers or "bourgeois" class. Ambitious monarchs welcomed the support of the townsmen, and used the taxes these "unprivileged" subjects paid into the royal treasury to bribe or to repress rebellious feudal barons.

Secondly, the Protestant Revolt, which began in 1517, reft half of Europe away from the Catholic Church. The monarchs took advantage of this weakening of the pope's authority. In countries where Protestantism triumphed, the lands, endowments, and income of the Catholic Church and Catholic monasteries were taken over by the secular rulers. Protestant monarchs thus acquired additional wealth with which to strengthen their power, while in countries that remained Catholic, the princes claimed a greater freedom from papal supervision in return for their loyalty.

A third factor that favored royal absolutism was the sharp rivalry among the princes themselves, who fought to enlarge their domains and increase the prestige of their dynasties. The wars of the sixteenth and seventeenth centuries made it clear that to win or even to survive in the new age an embattled state needed a strong centralized government which could exercise undivided authority. Kings could claim with some justice, when the state was in danger, that to oppose or even to criticize the royal authority was treasonable. The proverb, "Union is strength," had been quoted by Greek tyrants as early as the sixth century B.C. In the rising monarchical states of modern Europe, loyalty and obedience to the prince were emphasized as the cement that held classes and factions together and made a nation strong.

The centralized territorial state emerged as the dominant political unit of the modern era. The most powerful of these emerging states were controlled by hereditary monarchs who claimed to rule by divine right and denied that any earthly power had the authority to call them to account for their actions. The security of the state became the supreme concern of the ruler, and in the councils of government "reasons of state" overrode all other considerations. Stratagems that would have been judged immoral and dishonorable if undertaken for private advantage were regarded as justifiable in the service of the state. Monarchs broke contracts, repudiated debts, debased the coinage, seized the wealth of minority groups among their subjects, and resorted to summary arrest, imprisonment, and death to intimidate those rash enough to oppose the royal will. Machiavelli recognized the amoral nature of the new secular politics when he wrote in 1512, "Let a prince, therefore, take the surest courses he can to maintain his life and state: the means shall always be thought honorable."

From the fifteenth to the eighteenth century royal absolutism remained the most widely accepted form of government in Europe. The prince who exemplified the system most impressively was *le Grand Monarque,* Louis XIV of France. Louis lived from 1638 to 1715; he inherited the crown in 1643 when still only four and enjoyed a reign of seventy-two years. The royal power in France had been strengthened during the reign of Louis's father, Louis XIII, whose chief minister, Cardinal Richelieu, weakened the French Protestant minority and humbled the feudal nobility in his determination to make the king supreme. Richelieu's successor, Cardinal Mazarin, overcame further revolts against the royal authority. When he died in 1661, Mazarin left the young Louis XIV a secure throne, a subservient people, and a powerful army.

No successor was appointed in Mazarin's place. Instead, the twenty-two-year-old king announced that he would be his own first minister. He presided in person over the royal councils, kept the reins of government firmly in his own hands, and made himself the center of a glittering court. To his courtiers Louis XIV became *le Roi Soleil,* the sun king, and like the sun he illuminated the satellites around him with his reflected glory. Not only France but all Europe was dazzled by this hereditary monarch who discharged his responsibilities tirelessly and fulfilled his exacting role with dignity and decorum. Louis embodied the principle of monarchy in its most resplendent and awe-inspiring form. Other rulers imitated (so far as their means permitted) his vast and extravagant palace at Versailles, and neighboring nations lived in apprehension, knowing that peace or war depended on the whim of the king of France. The saying attributed to Louis, "*L'état c'est moi*" (I am the state), well summarizes his power, pride, and egotism.

In European history the period from 1660 to 1715, a period

of French ascendancy, is often distinguished as the age of Louis XIV. After a century of internal disorders, France enjoyed domestic peace and administrative stability. It had become the leading European power, and this French ascendancy, under an absolute monarch made royal absolutism appear the most brilliant and successful form of government. It might almost be said that although Louis XIV died in 1715 he threw his shadow across the remainder of the eighteenth century. His successor, Louis XV, could proclaim, as late as 1770, that "We hold our crown of God alone: the right to make laws appertains to us without dependence upon or share with another."

Not all nations were prepared to allow kings such absolute power. In 1581 the people of the Dutch Netherlands forswore their allegiance to Philip II of Spain and established the Dutch Republic. They justified their revolt on the ground that Philip had destroyed their liberties and treated them as slaves. When a prince becomes a tyrant, they argued, his subjects have the right to depose him.

In England the extreme claims James I put forward in defense of his royal authority (prerogative) angered many of his subjects. They allowed James to complete his reign (1603–1625), but when his son Charles I tried to rule in the same arbitrary spirit he stirred up a civil war. Defeated in battle and captured by his opponents, Charles went on trial before a special court which sentenced him to death by the headsman's ax. He died with courage and dignity on January 30, 1649.

Most Englishmen, however, remained royalists at heart. After eleven years of authoritarian rule under the successful general Oliver Cromwell, they welcomed back the son of "Charles the Martyr" as Charles II (1660–1685). But the limits of the royal prerogative had not yet been clearly settled. Charles' successor, James II (1685–1688), aroused such general opposition that he was deposed. The English Parliament gave the crown to his daughter Mary and her husband William of Orange, Stadtholder of the Dutch Republic. Thereafter England remained a limited monarchy, and subsequent rulers had to share their power with the elected representatives of the nation.

In most other European states, however, the power of the monarch remained absolute, in theory at least. Those who questioned the existing system were rebuked from the Scriptures—"The powers that be are ordained of God." Kings continued to rule by divine right, and resisted all suggestions that they share their prerogatives with their subjects. When the eighteenth century opened, most Europeans still accepted divine-right monarchy as the normal, the proper, the traditional form of government. When they prayed for reforms—and many reforms were desperately needed—they hoped to see their monarch heed their grievances and introduce the improvements himself. Only slowly and reluctantly did a minority come to feel that absolute monarchy itself might be one of the evils that must be abolished.

As Jefferson later observed, in the American Declaration of Independence, ". . . all experience hath shewn that mankind are more disposed to suffer, while evils are sufferable, than to right themselves by abolishing the forms to which they are accustomed." To understand the history of Europe in the eighteenth century and the programs of reform attempted by the "enlightened despots," it is important to keep two facts in mind: (1) History, as then taught, recorded few successful experiments in democratic government. (2) No large empire, indeed no large area, had ever been successfully governed as a republic.

It was logical, therefore, in the eighteenth century for reformers to think first of a royal edict as the surest instrument by which essential reforms might be accomplished. But it was also understandable that idealists, who had studied Greek and Roman history, should dream of a government in which the administration could be, as Pericles had said, "in the hands of the many and not of the few." The chapters that follow describe the hopes and aims of eighteenth-century reformers, the illusions they cherished, the programs they drafted, the experiments they undertook. Because the Europeans remained uncertain whether reform could best be achieved through despotism or through democracy, they vacillated between

these extremes. Only in America, where more favorable conditions prevailed, did the democratic ideal take root in the
eighteenth century and flourish without interruption or reversal. This discussion of the enlightened despots helps to
make clear why the Europeans proved less successful than the
Americans in their quest for liberty, and why they found it
more difficult to escape the force of tradition and the weight of
inherited customs.

1 The Philosophy of the Enlightenment

● *The Eighteenth Century* In European history the years from 1715 to 1789 constitute a relatively stable period between two more tumultuous eras. The grandiose ambitions and successive wars of Louis XIV ended with his death in 1715. Seventy-four years later, in 1789, the meeting of the States-General opened the turbulent era of the French Revolution and Napoleon. These two dates—1715 and 1789—are frequently accepted as marking off the eighteenth century as a coherent and recognizable period in European annals. It should be remembered, however, that the stream of history does not conform readily to a chronological pattern. To suggest definite dates for the beginning and end of a historical period is to ignore the continuity of history. The years 1715 and 1789 should be accepted only as approximate limits.

Nevertheless, it is possible to recognize characteristics in eighteenth-century Europe that give the age an individual and recognizable pattern. It was a century of dynastic intrigues, commercial rivalry, and intellectual ferment, when the stream of history pursued its slow-moving course toward the unexpected cataract of 1789. The years from 1715 to 1789 afford for the most part a chronicle of barren diplomacy and abortive wars. French art and arms, which had carried the fame of Louis XIV to the corners of Europe, suffered a slow decline under his successor, Louis XV, the Well-Beloved. Spain, ruled by a Bourbon after 1701, became a satellite of France and shared its decline. Italy was a collection of petty states under Hapsburg or Bourbon princelings. In Austria the Hapsburgs clung tenaciously to their disunited possessions and waning prestige. Alone of the Continental powers, Prussia and Russia made important gains: under Frederick the Great (1740–1786) the Prussian state doubled in area and population; and Russia, pressing forward on the Baltic, in Poland, and along the Danube, assumed for the first time a prominent role in European affairs.

These were developments fraught with important consequences for the nineteenth century, but in the eighteenth they scarcely disturbed the even tenor of the old regime. It was an age of professional diplomats and professional armies, a cynical age when every man was presumed to have his price and the ends sought were commercial gain or dynastic advantage, a formal age of order and etiquette and elegance. A hundred years earlier men had still rushed to battle in the heat of religious fervor, but religion and warfare alike had grown less intense and more conventionalized. The battalions of the eighteenth century marched and fought like automatons in the grip of a rigid discipline, until they went down to defeat before a horde of ragamuffins shouting the "Marseillaise."

Intellectually and culturally the period after the death of Louis XIV in 1715 was still dominated by French influences, a consequence of the ascendancy enjoyed by France during his lifetime. Richelieu's dream of making the king supreme in France and France supreme in Europe had come to realization in the glory of the Sun King. Even though the political hegemony of France was undermined by the Peace of Utrecht (1713), Paris remained throughout the eighteenth century the intellectual capital of Europe, and French the language of culture and diplomacy.

Slavishly the courts of Europe set themselves to imitate Parisian arts and manners. French literature was read from St. Petersburg to Lisbon; the French language bound the elegant everywhere into a cosmopolitan society, and the learned into a republic of letters. Beyond the environs of Paris everything ranked as provincial, and the cultured Europeans of other nations acknowledged two motherlands, their own and France.

The plastic mind of Europe was thus stamped with the impress of French genius at a time when such discipline might prove most salutary. In the service of the great writers of the seventeenth century the French tongue had become a medium of marvelous precision and elegance. Montaigne's humanism and rich classical traditions joined to Descartes' genius for organic unity of conception and Malherbe's love of a concise and lucid style had produced a language admirably fitted for the expression of eighteenth-century ideas in a form clear, logical, and axiomatic.

Two lines of thought converged in the eighteenth century to form one central strand, on the one hand the belief borrowed from Montaigne that the proper study of mankind is man, on the other the conviction of Descartes that the truth of an idea must be tested by its reasonableness. The philosophy woven from these two lines of thought was rationalism, a faith in reason that was almost a religion, and like a religion counted its prophets, its fanatics, and finally its martyrs. To the rationalists it seemed clear that men were intended by nature to be happy; unhappiness arose for the most part from error or from ignorance. If the rulers of states analyzed all problems in the light of pure reason, they would find a cure for all the ills of society. They were physicians who might, by prescribing a rational regimen, restore the body politic to a state of health.

This confident faith in man's power to improve his lot had come into Europe with the Renaissance: there is an interesting comparison to be drawn between the humanists of the sixteenth century and the rationalists of the eighteenth. Like the rationalists, the earlier scholars had also emphasized the need for social reforms and concurred in assigning to enlightened princes the duty of carrying them out; like the rationalists, they prophesied the dawn of a new age, a millennium in which reason would disarm prejudice and make man the master of his destiny.

It is a mistake to think of the French Revolution as introducing new principles into Europe. It only gave dynamic expression to ideas that had been developing throughout the century.

But although nearly all its reforms had been projected before, on paper at least, they had been introduced most often by monarchs or royal councilors and failed to enlist the backing of the people. Several decades before the French revolutionaries declared a war against all kings, the rulers themselves had prepared the way for it by familiarizing their subjects with the idea of reform and teaching them to desire better government. It is these attempts at social betterment made by the enlightened despots of the old regime, revolutions before the Revolution, that form the subject of this study. First, however, it is useful to consider the criticism that some of the leading thinkers and writers of the eighteenth century offered on existing conditions—criticism so effective that it undermined the foundations of the old regime.

• *Montesquieu, Voltaire, and Diderot* One of the earliest and most influential critics of eighteenth-century society was Charles de Secondat, Baron de Montesquieu (1689–1755). All Montesquieu's writing was inspired, directly or indirectly, by his search for the forms of law, custom, and government under which a people could live most freely and happily. His first literary work to win attention was his *Lettres persanes (Persian Letters)*, published in 1721. With satirical wit he described French society and the French court as two visiting Persians might have viewed them. This device permitted him to comment with candor and irreverence on royal despotism, the Catholic religion, and the folly and illogicality of many traditional practices. Montesquieu's second important work, *Considérations sur les causes de la grandeur des Romains et de leur décadence* (1734), emphasized his enthusiasm for ancient history and literature, his love of liberty, and his effort to analyze the virtues that distinguish a sound and well-organized society.

All these interests found a place in Montesquieu's third and most important work, *De l'esprit des lois (On the Spirit of Laws)*. This monumental study, published in 1748, embodied most of the major concepts that were to inspire political reformers throughout the remainder of the eigheenth century. The work manifested the customary respect still accorded the wisdom of the ancients. It stressed the prevalent faith in natural law. It praised and defended human dignity and individual liberty as good. It condemned despotism, slavery, and intolerance as evil. Finally, it assumed that laws and edicts, if they are to prove just and reasonable, must be in harmony with the nature, customs, and instincts of a people. Laws, by Montesquieu's definition, meant "the necessary relations arising from the nature of things." The intrinsic quality that all wise legislation must possess was that it be in harmony with the essential needs and character of a society. This intrinsic virtue constituted what Montesquieu termed the spirit *(esprit)* of the laws. His faith that such laws could be discerned by reason and applied with justice proves that this conscientious jurist was also a philosophical idealist.

Yet Montesquieu did not allow his preconceptions, or his faith in reason and natural law, to lead him to extremes, and this moderation marked him as a more cautious thinker than most of the later *philosophes*. He recognized that a human society is an exceedingly complex phenomenon and he did not advocate drastic or revolutionary measures as a cure for ancient ills. He explored many subjects which he judged relevant to the welfare of society and on three of these subjects he offered novel conclusions. First, he suggested that differences in climate affect the manners and morals of different peoples and should be taken into account by legislators who devise laws for them. Secondly, he noted that previous writers had commonly recognized three main forms of government—monarchy, aristocracy, and democracy. For these he substituted monarchy, in which the ruling principle was honor; despotism in which the ruling principle was fear; and democracy, in which the ruling principle was virtue. A third topic on which he displayed originality was his famous doctrine of the separation of powers. A sojourn in England (1729–1731) made him an admirer of the British form of government. He decided that the liberty of citizens can best be assured if the executive, legislative, and judicial powers in a state are separated and confided to different individuals or different bodies. No political concept of the eighteenth century exerted a greater influence on the legislators who were to draft a constitution for the United States and a succession of constitutions for revolutionary France.

In two further respects Montesquieu was representative of the *philosophes*. He knew how to use wit and irony with telling effect, and his *Persian Letters* have been described as the first book of the *Philosophe* Movement. "If the triangles made a god," one of the Persians remarks mockingly, "they would give him three sides." Such examples of irreverence alarmed the ecclesiastical censors and like all the leading *philosophes* Montesquieu suffered the penalty of their disapproval. When *De l'esprit des lois* was published (in Geneva) in 1748, it was attacked by clerics and conservatives in Paris and placed on the "Index of Prohibited Books" at Rome. Despite these attacks, or perhaps because of them, the work aroused such lively interest that twenty-two editions appeared within two years.

The most famous and prolific of the *philosophes* was Voltaire (assumed name of François Marie Arouet, 1694–1778), who has been called the embodiment of the Enlightenment. "Once upon a time," Georg Brandes wrote of him, "a bundle of nerves, charged with electricity, captivated Europe and enlightened it." Poet, satirist, dramatist, historian, essayist, critic, and inimitable correspondent, Voltaire wrote tirelessly for nearly three-quarters of a century. Like Montesquieu, he was familiar with the classics and was attracted by the information concerning other continents and civilizations which exploration and research had made available to eighteenth-century Europeans. Like Montesquieu, too, he hated intolerance and deplored the many obsolete customs and irrational laws that had become sanctified by tradition and were defended by unthinking prejudice. "Prejudices," he observed tartly, "are a fool's reasons."

Voltaire belies the view that most of the *philosophes* were impractical dreamers obsessed by a doctrinaire vision of a perfect society. Recent research has emphasized his realism in politics and his distrust of such dogmatic intellectual abstractions as natural law and natural rights. Although he wrote on natural law and defended it, his reference to it appears to have been a rhetorical device rather than a genuine expression of faith.[1] His realism also demonstrated itself in his business dealings, which he managed with hard-headed skill and acumen. At thirty-six he purchased shares in a government lottery which brought him a handsome profit. This fortune he increased by speculating in the wheat trade and in army supplies, and by driving shrewd bargains with his publishers.

Voltaire did not organize any system of philosophy or found a school of thought. His influence was a result of his humanity, his sensitivity to the inequities and injustices of his age, his lively and lucid style, and his tireless energy. In his later years he came to feel that intolerance, particularly religious intolerance, was the great obstacle to free discussion and enlightenment, and he popularized the phrase *écrasez l'infâme* (crush the infamous thing). In 1762 the execution of Jean Calas, a Protestant living in Toulouse, on the charge that he had murdered his son to keep him from becoming a Catholic, led Voltaire to defend the Calas family. His protests helped to force a retrial, and it was found that through passion and prejudice an innocent man had been put to death and other members of the Calas family unjustly punished.

"Everything I see," Voltaire wrote in 1764, "is sowing the seeds of a revolution that will inevitably come about and that I shall not have the pleasure of witnessing." The prediction became history. He died in May 1778, and in May, eleven years later, the French Revolution commenced. But Voltaire erred in imagining that he might have enjoyed witnessing it. The passion and fanaticism of the revolutionaries and the scenes of mob violence would have appalled him. Voltaire did not consider the common people capable of governing themselves. "The people should be guided, not informed," he asserted. "When the people take a hand in a debate, all is lost."

Another important writer of the eighteenth century, the

[1] Peter Gay, *Voltaire's Politics: The Poet as Realist* (Princeton, N. J., 1959), pp. 343-346.

gentle but indomitable Denis Diderot (1713–1784), was born in a quiet country town, the son of a cutler. Though educated at first for the priesthood, he rejected this calling and moved to Paris where he gained the degree of Master of Arts at nineteen. His interest in literature, languages, painting, mathematics, and science fitted him to be a publisher's assistant, and for some years he supported himself by translations which included a medical dictionary. Impressed by his energy, the publisher André le Breton invited him to translate and edit an English work, Chamber's *Cyclopaedia*, with the mathematician Jean Le Rond d'Alembert as coeditor. The project, as Diderot and D'Alembert conceived it, became the famous *Encyclopédie*, the greatest publishing achievement of the eighteenth century.

When they announced the *Encyclopédie* in 1750, the editors proposed a work of ten volumes, two of which were to be volumes of illustrations. Under Diderot's direction (1751–1772) the project expanded to twenty-eight volumes, and seven further volumes of addenda and tables raised the total to thirty-five by 1780. These thirty-five folio volumes, published over a period of thirty years, comprised the first edition of the justly celebrated *Encyclopédie*, the bible of the Enlightenment. Diderot wrote:

> The purpose of an encyclopedia is to gather together the knowledge scattered over the face of the earth, to explain its general scheme to men of our own time, to convey it to those who come after us, in order that the effort of past ages may not prove a fruitless labor for the ages that follow, and in order that our descendants, by becoming better informed, may therefore be happier and more virtuous, and we ourselves may not die without rendering a worthy service to the human race.

Diderot needed all the courage and inspiration he could draw upon to overcome frustration and opposition. The list of his proposed contributors, which included most of the leading *philosophes*, alarmed defenders of the old regime from the outset. By 1752, when the first two volumes of the *Encyclopédie* had appeared, the storm broke. A royal decree forbade further printing of these volumes and ordered existing copies confiscated. But the encyclopedists had friends in high places, including the king's mistress, Madame de Pompadour, who subsequently contributed an article—on *rouge*. Another influential friend was Lamoignon de Malesherbes, the official who issued or refused licenses to print new books. Malesherbes secretly warned Diderot, giving him time to hide the manuscripts, and intentionally omitted from the royal edict any reference to succeeding volumes, thus permitting the work to continue. A new wave of criticism gathered force in 1757; D'Alembert resigned; the *Encyclopédie* was condemned; and friends urged Diderot to flee. But he persisted in his labor and the storm abated; he did not discover until 1764 that the publisher, Le Breton, had softened a few passages that might have seemed particularly offensive to the critics.

Diderot's editorial labors have eclipsed his lesser works. His prolific pen turned out novels, dramas, satires, essays, and voluminous letters. As a critic of painting he was ahead of his time in taste and esthetic sensitivity; his lively and perceptive judgments set a standard for later art critics. Despite his industry he remained poor, and was aided in his later years by Catharine the Great of Russia. She bought his library but tactfully left it in Paris and paid him to care for it as her librarian. In 1773 Diderot visited St. Petersburg to thank her.

• *The Intellectual Temper of the Age*   If the leading thinkers of the eighteenth century placed an excessive trust in human reason, they felt this trust to be justified by the achievements of the men of science. Through the use of reason, Newton, in the previous century, had opened up the heavens and explained the movements of the stars by principles so clear that a child could understand them. Through the use of reason, the wandering comets, which in the Dark Ages had brought terror to the superstitious, had been shown to be harmless visitors, bound, like the stars, by the chains of unalterable law. Even the lightning —hurled, many devout people believed, by Satan in his role as Prince of the Powers of the Air—had been reduced by reason and experiment to a natural phenomenon: for it, as for the stars and comets, there existed invariable laws, and the human mind, having discovered these, could divert the fury of a bolt by a device as simple as a lightning conductor.

These triumphs of the scientific method led many writers to predict the dawn of an age wherein man, having discovered the laws of matter, would become the master of nature and of his destiny. Descartes had declared "all the things which we very clearly and distinctly conceive are true." This faith in the power of reason to discover truth, and the belief that truth when discovered would never prove self-contradictory or unreasonable, is known as rationalism.

To the extreme rationalists it seemed desirable that they overhaul every established belief or institution and reconstruct it in the light of pure reason; they held their formula to be a key that would unlock all mysteries. The defect of this optimistic philosophy lay in its first premise. It assumed tacitly that the emotions of the heart, the workings of the mind, the relations of society, and the business of government could be analyzed by the same methods and with the same ease as the physical sciences. Or to be more explicit, the rationalists failed to realize that the brilliant mathematical generalizations of the seventeenth century had been achieved in the physical sciences precisely because these were sciences of *measurement;* whereas the branches of knowledge pertaining more nearly to man, as psychology or medicine or anatomy, were still sciences of *classification,* and were not in a state to admit universal generalizations. This weakness of unbridled rationalism was pointed out by Abbé Mably in 1768. "Is society," he asked ironically, "a branch of physics?" For the consistent rationalist there was only one answer, but it was an answer that committed him to an unqualified materialism.

Medieval philosophers, supporting the medieval Church, had taught the duality of nature. There was a realm of matter, corrupt and temporary, and a realm of spirit, perfect and eternal. Many eighteenth-century rationalists tended to reverse this order: with them the world of matter became eternal and unchanging, while the glories of the heavenly kingdom paled like a candle in the sunlight. Such an overemphasis upon physical phenomena, the belief that nothing exists except matter and that the workings of the mind itself are due wholly to the operation of material agencies, constitutes the body of doctrines known as materialism.

A few extreme thinkers of the eighteenth century, steeped in this materialistic philosophy, came to doubt the world of spirits and even questioned the existence of God. From John Locke (1632–1704) these materialists accepted the maxim that nothing existed in the mind that had not come to it through the senses, and the senses could perceive only material objects. This theory of "sensationalism," which Locke advanced in *An Essay Concerning Human Understanding* (1690), won more attention in France than in England. Voltaire declared that a mind so wise, so methodical, so logical as Locke's had seldom, if ever, existed, and that Locke had exerted the greatest influence on philosophy since Plato.

It is the common fate of philosophers to have a few arresting concepts extracted from their teaching and overstressed, while the subtle definitions and qualifications of the context are ignored. Locke, whose thinking sometimes led others into materialism, was not a materialist himself, for he found a place in his philosophical system for a belief in God and the immortality of the soul. To Locke's mind, however, God was little more than a First Cause or Creator of the world, a God who never interfered with the machine he had constructed but left it to run itself much like a piece of clockwork. This position of compromise is known as deism.

Locke's ideas were carried further by David Hume (1711–1776), who dreamed of reducing the study of man, of politics, and history to exact sciences as Sir Isaac Newton had done for physics and astronomy. Some of Hume's essays, on natural religion, the existence of God, and the immortality of the soul, took so skeptical a turn that they were not published until after his death. His travels in France, however, and his correspondence with leading French thinkers made his speculations well known in that country. There his ideas, like Locke's, appealed to many agnostics, who found deism no better than a half-break with theology. A few of them went all the way and embraced a frank and unqualified atheism. To these radical materialists it appeared logical to conceive of matter as eternal and indestructible. The universe could then be viewed as a perpetual-motion machine that had always existed and the hypothesis of a Creator could be discarded.

The French physician Julien Offroy de La Mettrie (1709-1751) defended this mechanistic philosophy in several works, including his *Histoire naturelle de l'âme* (Natural History of the Soul), and *L'Homme Machine* (The Man Machine). An even more unattractive picture of the universe as the abode of dead and soulless matter was presented (1770) in the *Système de la nature* (The System of Nature) written by a wealthy baron, Paul Henri Dietrich d'Holbach (1723-1789). Two years later D'Holbach issued a second essay, *Bon sens ou idées naturelles opposées aux idées surnaturelles* (Common Sense or Natural Ideas Opposed to Supernatural Ideas). The German poet Goethe described in his reminiscences the revulsion he felt on reading D'Holbach's writing, which seemed to turn the smiling face of nature to the hue of a cadaverous specter.

It would be a mistake, however, to think that all or even a majority of the *philosophes* and reformers were materialists, rationalists, and atheists. It would be equally a mistake to believe that all of them were doctrinaire dreamers who abandoned reality to draft plans for syllogistic utopias. Even the most idealistic of them had to leave their ivory towers occasionally in order to cope with practical affairs. They lived in two worlds: the serene, harmonious, perfected society they idealized in their writings, and the turbulent disordered world of reality with its irrational customs and traditional inequalities.

As an example of the idealistic reformer who was also endowed with practical ability, one might consider the life of Pierre Samuel du Pont de Nemours. His early writings suggested an outlook intractably idealistic and doctrinaire. Yet later he established a printing and publishing house and also discharged various political offices with competence and moderation. His name, in fact, became more famous for its business than for its philosophical associations, for his youngest son founded a powder mill near Wilmington, Delaware, an enterprise that expanded into E. I. du Pont de Nemours and Company Inc. Or consider as a further example Anne Robert Jacques Turgot. Despite his attachment to physiocratic dogmas, he proved a remarkably successful Intendant of Limoges and a progressive Comptroller General of France. Even Jean Jacques Rousseau, that passionate apostle of the heart and its claims, could turn aside from his sentimental pilgrimage to draft thoughtful suggestions for the government of Poland and of Corsica. These practical activities of idealistic spirits should be kept in mind, to correct the impression that the *philosophes* were all impractical dreamers incapable of coping with the realities of life.

Nevertheless, the belief that the French Revolution and the ideas that inspired it were "the fault of Rousseau, the fault of Voltaire," does have some justification. The *philosophes*, like many eloquent writers before and since, failed to foresee the impact their phrases might have on the immature and the inexperienced. The oversimplified, seductive doctrine that all the evils and abuses of society could be remedied by drafting a code of laws based upon "the nature of things" captivated an entire generation. This utopian illusion found its most succinct expression in the French Constitution of 1793, which opens with the dogmatic statement: "The French people, convinced that neglect or defiance of the Natural Rights of man are the sole causes of human misery, have resolved to set forth . . . these sacred and inalienable rights in a solemn declaration."

• *Jean Jacques Rousseau* "Let us begin then by laying facts aside, as they do not affect the question." It is Rousseau speaking in his essay on the *Origin of Inequality* (1752), and the quotation suggests his singular egotism. Three years earlier he had won fame by the paradoxical argument that the progress of the arts and sciences had corrupted the morals of mankind. Now, in an equally paradoxical essay, he set out to show that social inequality was traceable to the same corrupting influence, the rise of civilization. Man, in his natural primitive state, Rousseau argued, had been a healthy, uncomplicated animal, responding to his natural instincts and impulses without premeditation. All animals, however, degenerate with domestication. "It is thus with man also; as he becomes sociable and a slave he grows weak, timid, and servile; his effeminate way of life totally enervates his strength and courage." In civilized society children were taught to conceal their thoughts and to curb the spontaneous expression of their emotions. Such training made them calculating, insincere, and hypocritical. "I almost dare to state," Rousseau wrote defiantly, "that reflection is an unnatural activity and the man who meditates is a depraved animal."

Rousseau's strange arguments not only gained attention, they won converts. His style possessed the supreme art of appearing artless—*ars est celare artem*—but Voltaire for one was not deceived by its air of guileless spontaneity. "No one," he wrote acidly to Rousseau, "ever employed so much ingenuity to persuade us to become animals. One is seized by an urge to run on all fours when one reads your work." Even Diderot, who had a generous nature, found he could not remain friendly with Rousseau. Their two minds, he protested, were separated by "the vast chasm between heaven and hell."

"Man is born free"; Rousseau declaimed, "and everywhere he is in chains. . . . How did this change come about?" Reformers all over Europe, irked by burdensome taxes and obsolete laws, were asking the same question. Rousseau undertook to explain the origin of government in his *Social Contract* (1762), the most influential of his works. The ideal state, as he pictured it, was a small republic, somewhat resembling the city of Athens in ancient times or in modern times the city of Geneva. In a free society, Rousseau argued, the citizens should be free to elect their own leaders and to dismiss those leaders whenever they proved incompetent or untrustworthy.

To defend democratic and republican ideas while living under a divine-right monarchy required courage. Rousseau had always been intensely sensitive and emotional, suspicious of everyone, and a prey to delusions of persecution. Like most of the *philosophes* he had trouble with the French censors and he entrusted his more controversial works to Dutch publishers. Warned in 1762 that an order had been issued for his arrest, he fled from France to Switzerland, soon found himself unpopular there, and journeyed to England in 1766, where he again quarreled with those who wished to help him. In 1770 he returned to Paris and died in 1778.

During his later years, Rousseau could not, by normal standards, be accounted sane. Yet his morbid sensitivity helped to explain his influence, for it made him acutely aware of social injustices. His lively imagination created images of a perfect society, and his seductive prose persuaded his readers that such a society could be achieved—that mankind could return to an Age of Gold. It is unnecessary to repeat that all the eighteenth-century reformers were stirred in some measure by the same hope, the same dream of a fairer world. When they looked back they saw the past as a long record of crimes and follies, but when they peered ahead they imagined that they could see a regenerated humanity living at peace, in harmony with nature:

> The world's unwithered countenance
> As fresh as on Creation's Morn.

• *The Old Regime* Everywhere the burden of the old regime weighed like an incubus upon Europe. The peasantry, though they were still oppressed by the obligations of the manorial system, had lost its benefits. As the national monarchies developed, kings had increased their authority until they curbed the aristocracy; but for the common people this change meant only the advent of a new and more efficient master. Wealth and power remained in the hands of the few. In France, with a population of twenty-five million, only less than three in a hundred belonged to the privileged classes. The rich devoured the poor, as the Marquis de Mirabeau[1] said, "like pikes in a pond." What the royal tax collector overlooked, the lord of the manor was swift to seize. For though the nobles stood between the people and the crown, it was only, in the bitter phrase of one writer, "as the hounds are between the hunter and the hare."

The peasants, the most hopeless victims of this system, were too crushed by their misfortunes to protest; it was the middle classes that raised most loudly the cry of social injustice. Wealthy bourgeois who envied the nobility; merchants whose profits were destroyed by illogical tariffs or swallowed up in endless lawsuits; journalists whose books were burned by stupid censors—all read Voltaire and shared his indignation at the existing regime. They demanded—and it was a bourgeois platform—equitable taxation, simplified laws, intellectual liberty, and religious toleration.

For such reforms there was a genuine practical need: they should have been attempted for the sake of governmental efficiency if for no other reason. But the privileged classes opposed any change in which they saw no advantage for themselves. The existing abuses had been hallowed by tradition; to destroy them it was necessary to destroy first the reverence with which they were regarded. For such a task Voltaire and his disciples were peculiarly fitted. Whenever they discovered some pious deception or miscarriage of justice they delighted to make a public scandal of it, to hold its perpetrators up to ridicule and laugh them out of court. Every grievance against the Church which came to their attention, every blunder of officialdom, provided them with an opportunity for turning loose the terrific stream of their ridicule, that astringent satire with which they planned to cleanse the Augean stables of Europe.

But as Alfred North Whitehead has amended, if men cannot live on bread alone, still less can they live on disinfectants.

[1] Victor Riqueti, Marquis de Mirabeau (1715–1789) was a French writer and political economist. He is not to be confused with his more famous son, Honoré Gabriel Riqueti, Comte de Mirabeau (1749–1791), the great orator of the French Revolution.

Ridicule might weaken abuses but it did not destroy them. Arguments had to be met by arguments, authorities by authorities. So the rationalists opposed the established order and the force of tradition with a natural order and the force of reason. Like all astute reformers they pretended that their program offered no new departure but a return to first principles. The government had grown corrupt, the laws were in confusion, virtue had decayed, religion was sunk in ritual. It was necessary to "purify society," to "destroy the cancerous abuses," to "cut off the gangrened limb." Then the body politic, under the direction of skilful physicians, would return to a state of health.

On every side the *philosophes* found examples of inefficiency, confusion, devotion to precedent, whereas what they admired was *lumière,* enlightenment, clarity, method, order. Too often the governments which were maintained to regulate the affairs of nations could not organize their own departments. Finance ministers cast up the accounts of a state with a slovenliness that would have ruined a third-rate banking house. Their budgets and balance sheets were often matters of pure guesswork; they had no accurate data for calculating the resources of a nation, no adequate means for collecting the taxes, no method for regulating the expenditure.

Such conditions the critics of government quite rightly denounced as irrational. When they demanded that the institutions of society should be reorganized in accordance with natural laws, they were only voicing in borrowed philosophic terms the desire of all sane men for greater efficiency in the management of the state. The reasoning of philosophers about nature and society was harmless enough in itself and little likely to disturb the established order. Indeed, many of the political writers of the eighteenth century preferred to confine themselves entirely to brilliant generalizations, and to leave specific grievances alone. But in an age so full of abuse and discontent there were plenty of bolder minds ready to give to airy nothings a local habitation and a name, and to convert abstract formulas about natural law and natural right into sharp-edged weapons for hacking at the tree of privilege and the chains of superstition. No handful of intellectuals, however busily they sowed the wind, could have stirred to its depths a satisfied and prosperous society; but the people of Europe in the eighteenth century were few of them either prosperous or happy.

• *Confusion of Juristic and Scientific Law* The key to eighteenth-century political thinking is the idea of natural law. Behind the variety of nature the *philosophes* felt was a rational order, a kind of mathematical pattern. The idea was not new. "God geometrizes," Plato said, and he sought for reality in certain ultimate Ideas pre-existent in the mind of God—"Types, whose earthly copies were the foolish broken things we knew." It had been a precept of the Stoics likewise that "nature has established rational principles for all that is": the idea, embedded in the philosophy of Roman law,[1] had been borrowed by Aquinas and by Dante after him. But in the eighteenth century the concept suddenly took on a new vitality. For reason, following the inductive method, had begun to uncover these natural laws and to find in them a beauty, a simplicity, a self-sufficiency beyond all expectations. There remained only the task of reconciling life to its pattern and remodeling human institutions according to nature's pre-established harmony.

Since the reorganization of society on the basis of these principles could best be brought about by effective legislation, the rationalists turned their attention to the problem of legal reform. The need for a single simplified code of law in each state had been evident since the sixteenth century, yet in France alone, before the Revolution, justice was administered according to three hundred and sixty different codes. No one could determine where the jurisdiction of manorial courts ended, where that of the provincial *parlements* began, or what pretext might authorize the intervention of the royal *intendants*. So justice lagged and lawyers flourished, while the business

[1] See above, pp. 4–5.

of life was tied up by a mass of contradictory legislation and conflicting decisions.

For all this the *philosophes* had a simple solution. The function of the legislator was not to make laws but to discover them. Men in society no less than bodies in space were subject to rational principles; the formulation of these was to be the miracle which would bring harmony out of chaos. Since the new legal formulas would possess the same lucidity and command the same acceptance as the axioms of Euclid, they would establish in the affairs of government a mathematical precision. This miscalculation, this confusion of juristic with scientific law, could only have occurred in a century obsessed, like the eighteenth, with the triumphs of mathematics. It made society, as Mably had pointed out, a branch of physics.

The codification of a new table of law was to be the first step in the *philosophes'* program of reform. These laws were to be few in number, based upon natural principles, and expressed in such simple language that the wayfaring man, though a fool, might not err therein. The more optimistic theorists even hoped that such a code, like the legislation of the Utopians, would possess in itself a rectifying quality, so that the citizens enjoying its benefits "could not choose but be good." They believed that the institution of wise laws would produce a spirit of harmony and cooperation in society, an improved morale, unique and unmistakable, which they distinguished by the term Virtue, and which Plato had defined as "a kind of health and beauty and good condition of the soul." In the nineteenth century a similar hope inspired many democratic leaders to dream that universal manhood suffrage would harmonize the interests of all classes and assure social harmony. It is a perennial ideal.

Stripped of its idealistic elements the plan for judicial reform, like those projected in education, in agriculture, in sanitation, possessed excellent possibilities. There was, however, another problem more pressing than these. The sinews of government, as of war, are sound finances; the primary problem of statecraft, most absorbing to king and people alike, was the task of securing the economic welfare of the nation. To discharge its functions a government had to command an adequate revenue; to meet the necessary taxation the people had to be rendered reasonably prosperous. This vital connection between economics and government was developed into a philosophy towards the middle of the eighteenth century by a group of French thinkers who have become famous in history as the *économistes* or physiocrats.

• *The Physiocrats* The term *physiocrate* though coined by Quesnay, did not come into general use until the nineteenth century; his followers preferred the title *économistes*. But physiocracy, implying as it does government according to natural order, expresses so much more definitely the central doctrine of this school that it has superseded the earlier term.

François Quesnay (1694–1774) was court physician to Louis XV, but his chief interest lay in economic and agricultural problems. In 1756 and 1757 he contributed to the *Encyclopédie* of Diderot two articles, on "*Grains*" and "*Fermiers*" in which he set forth the principles of a new system of political philosophy. His ideas were adopted with enthusiasm by the young Du Pont de Nemours who believed with the faith of an acolyte that the true method of reforming society had been revealed at last. He sought to popularize Quesnay's system in a work which he published under the ambitious title *De l'origine et du progrès d'une science nouvelle* (On the origin and progress of a new science).

At the basis of Quesnay's thinking was a belief in natural order. "Laws," he affirmed, "are rules of justice, morality, and conduct, applicable to all and each. Men and governments never made them, nor ever could; they can only recognize them as conforming to the supreme reason which governs the universe." In the discovery and application of these natural principles lay the secret of reforming society. Du Pont de Nemours wrote:

There is one essential route by which we can approach, as nearly as it is possible to do, the problem of human association and the formation of political bodies. There is a natural order, necessary and universal, which determines the basic and constitutional laws of all societies . . . an order which can never be forsaken without inviting the dissolution of society and the complete destruction of the human race.

The fame of the physiocrats did not consist, however, in the belief that nature held a pattern which man-made laws should copy. Such ideas were the common property of almost all eighteenth-century thinkers. The peculiar success of Quesnay, according to his followers, lay in the fact that he had *discovered* and *isolated* those basic laws of society upon which all else depended. He was the Newton of the social system, the originator of that "new science" which Du Pont de Nemours was ready to celebrate.

If the achievement of this ugly little man, whom his disciples likened to Socrates, had been verifiable, all Europe would have been ready to attend his triumph. But the results proved disappointing. Quesnay published some general maxims of government and accompanied them by an economic chart, but the maxims lacked that compelling simplicity which natural laws were supposed to possess; and the *Tableau économique* remained incomprehensible to most readers, even though he supplemented it by seven appendixes and the Marquis de Mirabeau explained it in three ponderous volumes. Voltaire poured ridicule upon the members of the school; Abbé Mably challenged their conception of a state with his own fantastic and idealized Sparta; and theorists who preferred to amuse themselves with the construction of airy utopias shrank from the labor of grappling with the abstruse economic formulas upon which the physiocrats based their philosophy.

It is, in fact, as economic theorists rather than as political philosophers that the physiocrats deserve consideration. Though many of their most cherished axioms were wrong, even a wrong axiom may have its uses as a weapon of destruction in the hands of a reformer. Eighteenth-century writers on political economy, such as Richard Cantillon who died in 1734, and Vincent de Gournay (1712–1759), had ventured to attack the prevailing mercantilist or bullionist theory of trade. This theory taught that to remain prosperous a state should preserve a favorable balance of trade, that is, it should make the value of its exports exceed that of its imports. The excess value of the goods exported would be paid for in gold by the country receiving them, thus directing a steady stream of bullion to the state which successfully adhered to mercantilist principles. The physiocrats, following in the footsteps of Cantillon and Gournay, raised a number of objections to this system. The wealth of a state, they insisted, could not be increased by accumulating gold, but only by the mass of its agricultural and mineral products unconsumed in the process of production. To this annual increase in the sum of raw material available for human use they applied the term *produit net* (net profit), and they made it the basis of a new theory of political economy.

The economic teaching of the physiocrats appeared fantastic to a majority of their contemporaries and exerted little influence in France before the Revolution. Across the Channel, however, the Scotsman Adam Smith, who knew members of the physiocratic school, was analyzing the same problems, and the publication in 1776 of his famous treatise "An Inquiry into the Nature and Causes of the Wealth of Nations" was in many respects a vindication of physiocratic theories. Like the pupils of Quesnay, Smith condemned mercantilism and exalted labor as the source of wealth and the standard of value; but he was less obsessed than they by prepossessions regarding natural law and other abstract philosophical principles, and his writings had a wider influence and a greater value than theirs.

Almost all the *philosophes* were distinguished by an irritating assurance and a prodigious conceit which made them at times more than a little wearisome; but the physiocrats were perhaps the most dreary of the lot. Monarchs like Frederick II of Prussia (1740–1786) and Catharine II of Russia (1762–1796), who understood the difficulties of practical administration, sometimes listened with a strained patience to the pedantic lectures of these philosophers whom they, and all Europe, delighted to honor. "They sing their own praises," confessed Gustavus III of Sweden (1771–1792), "with as much complacency as ever their admirers could do." And Frederick wrote in 1774, "Diderot is at St. Petersburg, where the Czarina has overwhelmed him with honors; but they say that his arguments fill her with weariness for he does nothing but repeat the same things over and over again." When Catharine was planning a new code of laws for the Russian people she invited Mercier de la Rivière to her court, but one encounter with the dogmatism of the physiocratic mind sufficed to satisfy her.

"Can you tell me, Sir," she asked, "the best way to govern a state well?"—"There is only one, Madame," replied the pupil of Quesnay, "it is to be just, that is, to maintain order and to enforce the laws."—"But on what basis should the laws of an empire repose?"—"On one alone, Madame, the nature of things and men."—"Exactly, but when one wishes to give laws to a people, what rules indicate most surely the laws which suit it best?"—"To give or make laws, Madame, is a task which God has left to no one. Ah, what is man, to think himself capable of dictating laws to beings whom he knows not, or knows so imperfectly? And by what right would he impose laws upon beings whom God has not placed in his hands?"—"To what, then, do you reduce the science of government?"—"To study well, to recognize and manifest, the laws which God has so evidently engraven in the very organization of man when he gave him existence. To seek to go beyond this would be a great misfortune and a destructive undertaking."[1]

● *Enlightened Despotism* As champions of individual liberty the physiocrats deplored all arbitrary methods of government; but they believed none the less that the central authority of the state had to be preserved. Power might be a good or an evil thing depending on its use, but it could not be discarded or dissipated. "There should be one sovereign authority superior to all the individuals of a society," Quesnay had declared. "The idea of several authorities in the same state," added Du Pont de Nemours, "suggests nothing less than an absurdity." To these philosophers it seemed better that the promulgation of the laws should be entrusted to a monarch rather than to a legis-

[1]Thiébault, *Souvenirs de vingt ans de séjour à Berlin*, 2nd ed. III, pp. 167-168. Quoted in H. Higgs, *The Physiocrats*, (London 1897), p. 88

lature; for if all the legislators thought alike, one head would do as well as many; whereas if the legislators differed, it would prove that they were not equally enlightened. So with the exception of one of two of their number—Mirabeau, Morellet— the physiocrats agreed in favoring that form of government which is known as enlightened despotism.

The word despot, however, they wished to strip of all ugly connotations. The true despot ought to be the servant of his people, exercising his power solely for their good, recognizing their welfare as his own. There were two methods by which society might be regenerated. One, a slow and laborious method, depended upon the gradual spread of enlightenment until it reached all classes and individuals in a state. The second, promising swifter results, might be set in action if a wise prince, a modern Lycurgus, instituted at one sweep the necessary laws of social harmony. An enlightened ruler, provided his power were adequate, could reorganize and revivify the life of a nation by a few well-reasoned edicts, and thus earn the gratitude of his people. The concept of the philosopher-prince was as old as Plato and had played its part in Roman and in Chinese history. Diderot reaffirmed the ideal in the *Encyclopédie* when, after discussing the term *philosophe*, he added, "graft a prince onto such a philosopher and you will have the perfect ruler."

Such a prince could make the title of despot glorious. Since his ordinances would, on their own merits, win the acceptance of all right-thinking men, they would scarcely require the backing of his absolute authority. Mercier de la Rivière wrote:

Euclid is the true type of despot. The geometrical axioms which he has transmitted to us are genuine despotic laws; in them the legal and the personal despotism of the legislator are one and the same thing, a force evident and irresistible; and for that reason the despot Euclid has for centuries exercised his unchallenged sway over all enlightened peoples.

For the first time in history the art of government might be raised to an exact science, and the affairs of men regulated, it was hoped, with perfect order and efficiency. An opportunity unique and enviable was offered the monarchs of the eighteenth century: it was to be their privilege to reorganize society in accordance with the new discoveries. "It is an obligation laid upon sovereigns," proclaimed Du Pont de Nemours, "to promulgate by positive ordinances the natural and essential laws of the social order."

Thus royal despotism in Europe entered its third and final stage. The idea had won acceptance that kings existed for the benefit of their people, not the people for the benefit of the king. In the Reformation era a ruler like Philip II imposed his will and his religion upon his subjects, and held himself responsible to God alone. This period of confessional absolutism was followed in the seventeenth century by the brilliant, courtly despotism of Louis XIV, well suggested by the saying *L'état c'est moi*. But the eighteenth century introduced a new pattern of kingship, and the magnificence of the Grand Monarch was eclipsed by the restless figure of Frederick the Great wielding his unlimited authority not as a divine right but as a trust devolving upon him as the first servant of the state.

Frederick was the most brilliant and the most successful of the eighteenth-century despots, and he served as a model for his contemporaries. Throughout Europe earnest and ambitious princes strove to imitate him, and to apply the principles of the Enlightenment to secure the welfare of their subjects. Too scant a justice has been accorded these benevolent despots of the old regime. They threw themselves into the work of reform with diligence and zeal, spurred on by the double motive of humanitarianism and national ambition. They strove in one century to atone for the mistakes their ancestors had committed in five: the eighteenth century was, in Lord Acton's phrase, "the monarchs' age of repentance."

Young rulers prepared themselves for the duties of kingship by reading the works of the *philosophes*, enthusiastically, but it is to be feared, uncritically. Furthermore, they corresponded with one another in order to compare their reform programs.

Setting aside minor differences they expected to find the principles of good government of universal application and they strove to see who should first discover and apply them. "Here is the summary," Du Pont de Nemours had suggested modestly in closing his *Origine et progrès d'une science nouvelle*—

Here is the summary of that teaching which, in accordance with the nature of man, reveals the laws essential to a government made for man and proper to man in all climates and all lands; to the society which has existed in China these four thousand years under the Tropic of Cancer, and to that government which the genius of a great empress is raising even now for the happiness of her subjects amid the frozen wastes of the North. . . .

This optimistic passage was penned by Du Pont de Nemours in 1767. It was a period of high hopes for the *philosophes*. In St. Petersburg Catharine had just issued her instructions for the codification of Russian law; Frederick the Great was devoting all his genius and energy to the rehabilitation of the Prussian state; Joseph II, recently elected Holy Roman Emperor and co-regent with his mother Maria Theresa, was preparing a list of extraordinary reforms against the day when he should assume sole authority in the Hapsburg dominions. The Spanish people were enjoying the enlightened rule of Charles III, while in Portugal the reforming minister Pombal was at the height of his power. It seemed as if a single generation might witness the reconstruction of European society. "There is no prince in Europe," wrote Diderot confidently, "who is not also a philosopher."

• *The Conflict of Rationalism and Religion*   "Those who rely on the dogmas of the theologians are relying upon weathercocks that turn with every wind," wrote Pierre Bayle (1647–1706). This French philosopher and critic anticipated the *philosophes* in his attacks on religious dogmatism and his pleas for religious toleration. A journal which he edited from 1684 to 1687, *Nouvelles de la république des lettres*, and a *Dictionnaire historique et critique*, which he published in 1697, reflected his growing skepticism on religious questions. His erudition, his cool logic, and his playful irony helped to dissolve respect for

Christian orthodoxy, and his argument that it is possible to be moral without being religious aroused sharp controversies.

Fifty years after Bayle's death his skeptical arguments were familiar to all the leading *philosophes*. "I am happy, Sire," the French scientist D'Alembert wrote Frederick the Great of Prussia, "to find myself in agreement with Your Majesty as to the hollowness and futility of metaphysics." By metaphysics the enlightened thinkers of the eighteenth century meant all speculations about God and the soul, and they felt it was a waste of time to discuss these subjects which they considered unknowable. There was a growing tendency among all classes to forsake the mysteries of religion for more secular and more congenial studies.

For this irreligious mood the teaching of the *philosophes* was partly responsible. D'Holbach reflected the attitude of a great many agnostics when he wrote in the *Système de la nature:*

The moment a man begins to perplex himself with ideas of God and religion, ideas which he can understand nothing whatever about, his reasoning leads him wildly astray, or else he becomes the victim of sophistries. Yet even when he comprehends not a word of what is asserted in such matters he will credit his teachers with a complete understanding of them; and the latter do not fail to assure him that the path of certitude is to accept their words with blind and implicit faith. Should he decline to believe what he is told, they threaten him with the fury of a splenetic Shade, and by such an argument, which begs the whole question at issue, they close everyone's mouth. . . . Thus the priestly authority settles once and for all a matter which is of no great profit to anyone—except the priests.

The power of the Church had waned since the previous century, when Giordano Bruno perished at the stake, and Galileo, knowing the stars in their courses would fight on his side, had bowed before the Inquisition.[1] Yet theology still had a subtle

---

[1]Giordano Bruno (1548-1600), an Italian philosopher and skeptic, was burned by the Inquisition at Rome in 1600 for maintaining among other doctrines the theory of Copernicus that the earth revolves about the sun. Ten years later Galileo (1564-1642) demonstrated the truth of the Copernican hypothesis by telescopic observations, but the Inquisition forced him to deny his discoveries.

capacity to escape from the nets of reason, and its opponents feared it would continue to do so as long as the Church controlled the education of children. Not even the mind of René Descartes, (1596–1650), great rationalist though he was, had been agnostic enough to liberate itself from the influences that shaped its earliest development. "Being given assuredly to understand," he wrote, "that the revealed truths which lead to heaven are above our comprehension, I did not presume to subject them to the impotency of my Reason." This allegiance of Descartes to the teaching of the Church was more than a mere lip service prescribed by caution. He never liberated himself from the theological concepts of his Jesuit teachers. The physical world and man's physical body, he concluded, obey physical laws—"The rules of nature are identical with the rules of mechanics." But man's soul was something different from, something superior to, its earthly prison. The lower animals, which had no souls, were for Descartes nothing more than machines, whereas man, whose body, like that of the animals, was a machine, also possessed a soul.

To convinced agnostics all such reverence for religious dogmas seemed mere unverifiable superstition. They hesitated, however, to attack the doctrines of the theologians too frankly lest they find their writings condemned by the censors. To guard against the charge of impiety they frequently prefaced their critical attacks by a preliminary obeisance to the Church and to Christian teaching, knowing that sophisticated readers would follow the direction of their thinking and appreciate the irony of their exposition.

Thus Voltaire, in his *Dictionnaire philosophique*, contrasts Christianity with the natural religion the *philosophes* admired.

I shall not discuss our own [religion] here. It alone is good, necessary, demonstrable... But if it were possible for the human mind to conceive a second (I will not say at all approaching ours, but better than all other creeds of the world together) what would that religion be like? Would it not urge us to worship the Supreme Being, unique, infinite, eternal, who created the world? . . . Would it not reject the dogmas invented by pride which are subjects of endless disputations, and teach

instead a pure morality about which there could be no dispute? . . .
Would it not enjoin us to serve our neighbors through love of God, instead of persecuting and butchering them to his greater glory? And
would not such a faith, which by tolerance toward all could earn the
goodwill of all, be alone capable of uniting mankind into a nation of
brothers?

The high water mark of success in the rationalist assault
upon the Church was reached in 1773 when Pope Clement
XIV was persuaded to suppress the Society of Jesus. There
were several reasons why the Jesuits should have been singled
out for attack. Organized first in 1540 they had made themselves the "spearhead" of the Catholic or Counter Reformation,
and had become the most powerful single factor in checking
heresy and defending the papal authority. The Society of Jesus
exacted the highest degree of discipline and obedience from its
members, for its founder, Ignatius Loyola, planned that his
followers should be soldiers and, if need be, martyrs of Christ.
He prayed that persecution should be their lot and they earned
it by an unflinching devotion to the interests of the papacy and
an unremitting contest against heretics and freethinkers. In
the eighteenth century the enemies of the Jesuits were more
numerous than ever before. Even the popes were suspicious of
their powers, and members of other religious orders resented
their independence and the secrecy of their organization. Their
great influence, because it was often exerted through hidden
channels, appeared to their enemies peculiarly sinister. Kings
suspected them of encouraging the people to believe it was
legitimate to murder a tyrant; the people attributed unpopular
edicts of the princes to the influence of Jesuit confessors. To the
philosophes with their love of religious freedom the Jesuits were
a symbol of that spirit of dogmatism in the Church which
they were fighting against above all else.

In France the growing hatred of the Jesuits resulted in their
expulsion from the kingdom in 1764. Although the members
were pledged to poverty, they had long indulged in commercial
ventures which brought the Society into discredit, for they used
their privileges, especially in the American colonies, to extend

their trading activities, and amassed excessive wealth. Yet when, in 1755, a Jesuit mission in Martinique became bankrupt, leaving debts of two million *livres*, the Society repudiated any responsibility. The resulting litigation in the French courts excited an extraordinary animosity against the Jesuits until in 1764 they were driven out of France. Their expulsion from Spain and Portugal is recorded elsewhere.[1] Finally, in 1773, Pope Clement XIV was induced to revoke their charter, and the dissolution of the Society was hailed as a victory by leaders of the Enlightenment throughout Europe. In their taste of power the rationalists showed little compassion for the deported fathers; almost alone Frederick the Great of Prussia displayed concern over their sufferings and offered them a refuge in his dominions. "As for me, heretic that I am," he wrote D'Alembert when he heard the Society was to be scattered, "I shall take the credit of collecting the debris in Silesia, and not add to their misfortunes."

In the society of the future, as anticlerical reformers liked to picture it, the clergy would lose their influence in the schools and their places would be taken by laymen. Even religion itself was to become a civic activity, the handmaid of good government, its function being to support the state and spread a spirit of harmony among all classes. Europe's clashing sects were to be supplanted by a religion of nature which would unite the human race in the rites of a simple cult. To many rationalists it seemed obvious that the Supreme Being, who had established harmonious laws to govern the movements of the farthest star, could never have intended the relations of men to remain in chaos. Left to itself, they thought, the human reason could soon discover the laws of social harmony. A new generation, born into a world purged of sectarian controversy and priestly machinations, should know the truth and the truth would make them free. Since the child's mind was a *tabula rasa* it would accept the principles of natural religion because of their sweet reasonableness. Then all men would

[1] See Chap. 3.

live together in amity, recognizing the right of each to life, liberty, and the pursuit of happiness. They held these truths to be self-evident.

• *The Noble Savage*   In every civilized age a few impatient souls, oppressed by the involvements and complexities of their society, long to return to a more simple life. Greek and Roman poets contrasted the leisurely, uncomplicated existence of the shepherd or farmer with the hurried, anxious days of the townsman or courtier. In the fifteenth and sixteenth centuries the Renaissance writers revived this pastoral tradition. Sir Philip Sidney called his fanciful romance *Arcadia*, and Shakespeare, in *As You Like It*, pictured life in the Forest of Arden as rural bliss.

> Hath not old custom made this life more sweet
> Than that of painted pomp? Are not these woods
> More free from peril than the envious court?

The fiction that those who lived close to nature enjoyed a happier, more tranquil existence led in turn to the fantasy that savages, free from the constraints of civilization, enjoyed greater freedom and equality than the cultured Europeans. The British poet laureate, John Dryden, in 1670, gave one of his characters the boastful lines:

> I am as free as nature first made man
> Ere the base laws of servitude began
> When wild in woods the noble savage ran.

This concept of the "noble savage" and of his superiority to his corrupted, effeminate civilized brothers captivated many eighteenth-century reformers. Dreaming of a return to the Garden of Eden, to an Age of Gold, they persuaded themselves that they could find lingering traces of the lost paradise among primitive tribes or in country hamlets. Having borrowed their happy illusion from literature—from Theocritus, Virgil, and Tacitus—they clung to it with tenacity, preferring to cherish a dream rather than investigate the harsh actuality.

Some English writers, it is true, showed a healthy skepticism regarding the nobility of savages and the charms of rustic solitude. Thomas Hobbes argued that a man living in a state of nature would find his life "solitary, poor, nasty, brutish, and short." Samuel Johnson, when told that South Sea islanders lived idyllic lives, rejected the notion with the peremptory rebuke, "Don't cant in defense of savages!" The poet Thomas Gray, in his *Elegy Written in a Country Churchyard*, concluded that "the rude forefathers of the hamlet" had led obscure, illiterate lives without education or opportunity.

> Knowledge to their eyes her ample page,
> Rich with the spoils of time, did ne'er unroll;
> Chill penury repressed their noble rage,
> And froze the genial currents of the soul.

William Cowper, who grew up in the countryside and later served as a commissioner of bankrupts in London, likewise understood that poverty often numbs but seldom ennobles those who suffer it.

> The poor, inured to drudgery and distress,
> Act without aim, think little and feel less,
> And nowhere, but in feigned Arcadian scenes,
> Taste happiness, or know what pleasure means.

These sober judgments had the ring of truth but they did not destroy the idyllic myths that poets and painters spread abroad with their "feigned Arcadian scenes." A sentimental generation continued to cherish romantic illusions about the happy, tranquil life of shepherds and savages although these illusions contradicted irreducible brute facts.

● *Romance and Reality*   It is an easy matter to point out that the ideal state projected by these theorists was an impossible one. Philosophers are for the most part bookish men, averse to all forms of tumult or violence. The society planned by the idealists was to be orderly, harmonious, and static;

since there can be no advance beyond perfection, they omitted the elements of conflict and progress and evolution. Even when they urged a return to nature, they never envisaged it in a savage or primitive mood. What they had in mind was a landscape of Watteau—a sylvan Arcady where storms never ventured, and all uncouth passions and destructive forces were softened by the touches of a deft technique. Through the use of some similar magic—a few swift strokes, a little dexterous foreshortening—they hoped to resolve the conflicts of society into a picture of order and elegance. Then they would lead a regenerate humanity back to Arcadia—an Arcadia as timeless as a dream or a painting, from which they had banished all unreasoned impulses and infinite horizons.

The doctrinaire mind always betrays itself in the attempt to wrench reality into agreement with an arbitrary pattern. Disquieted at times by the cold perfection of their ideal state, the idealists sought to fit humanity into the picture, only to behold their categories crack beneath the strain. From this predicament they escaped—in theory at least—by the dogma of human perfectibility. The children of the future, better educated, purged of ancient follies and prejudices, would know how to venerate the philosophy of enlightenment; with a new generation reared under new and perfected institutions, mankind would come into its heritage.

How completely the faith in perfected institutions captivated some of the revolutionary generation may be gathered from the writings of Saint-Just. This young colleague of Robespierre, who helped to draft the French Constitution of 1793, recorded the tenets of his creed in terse unequivocal phrases.

It has always seemed to me that the social order was implicit in the very nature of things and required nothing more from the human spirit than care in arranging the various elements; that a people could be governed without being made thralls or libertines or victims thereby; that man was born for peace and liberty and became miserable and cruel only through the action of insidious and oppressive laws. And I believe therefore that if man be given laws which harmonize with the dictates of nature and of his heart he will cease to be unhappy and corrupt...[1]

Even the sober Wordsworth, who visited France for a year (1791–92) when he was twenty, responded to the revolutionary spirit and to the prevailing faith that society could be transformed by wise legislation.

> Bliss was it in that dawn to be alive
> But to be young was very heaven! - Oh! times,
> In which the meagre, stale forbidding ways
> Of custom, law and statute, took at once
> The attraction of a country in romance! [2]

When the Revolution threw down the gates and a turbulent humanity poured into Arcadia the whole framework collapsed like the theatrical setting it was. Few figures in history are more tragic than the idealists of 1793 and 1794, who sought like Robespierre to hold together the ruins of a syllogistic paradise, or learned with the Girondists that the genie of revolution, once unloosed, could not be persuaded back into its bottle. These men could not live their dream, but they did not hesitate to die for it; after them came Napoleon, to pour contempt upon the ideologists and to an ounce that the romance of the Revolution was over.

Napoleon was not the first to detect that the eighteenth century ideal of a perfected society was at best a romantic dream. The influence of the *philosophes* and publicists who hoped to reform society had never been as effective as they thought. Most of the princes who flattered the *philosophes* and expressed admiration for their programs were concerned with very real administrative problems, not with abstract ideals. The pressing duty of those princes was to govern and

---

[1] Louis Antoine Léon de Saint-Just, *Oeuvres complètes*, edited by Charles Vellay (Paris, 1908) Vol. 1, p. 419.

[2] William Wordsworth, "French Revolution as it appeared to enthusiasts at its commencement."

defend their states. If a proposed reform promised to make their army more efficient, increase their revenue, or strengthen their authority they were happy to consider it. If they could gild their decrees by attributing them to the enlightened spirit of the age, this too they were happy to do. But neither the princes nor their ministers could afford to forget that "Politics is the doctrine of the possible, the attainable." This truth, which Bismarck emphasized in the nineteenth century, was equally true in the eighteenth and the seventeenth. Basically the policies of the enlightened despots were motivated by reasons of state, although it was always expedient to find moral and idealistic arguments to embellish and disguise them.

As Richelieu remarked, *Savoir dissimuler est le savoir des rois* (To know how to dissemble is the craft of kings).

2 Frederick II, Joseph II, and Catharine II

FREDERICK THE GREAT

● *Austria and Prussia,* 1740-1763   With the death of Frederick William I, on May 21, 1740, the throne of Brandenburg-Prussia passed to a young prince, twenty-eight years of age, who had been his father's despair. The fondness of the youthful Frederick for such impractical pursuits as flute-playing and French versification drove Frederick William to employ Spartan severities in an effort to reform his son. He drilled him doggedly in the details of civil and military administration, left him a well-filled treasury, and died with the hope that Frederick, despite his effeminate inclinations, might prove not wholly a disgrace to the House of Hohenzollern.

The death of Frederick William was followed five months later by that of the Hapsburg emperor, Charles VI. The House of Austria at this period ruled over some twenty-five million people for the Hapsburgs were masters of the Danube Valley, Lombardy, Swabia, and the Austrian Netherlands. The Bourbons ruled France, Spain, Naples, and the Two Sicilies. In the predominance of these two dynasties the young Frederick recognized a danger to the smaller states of Europe. A third power was needed, he felt, to counterbalance the other two; and he prepared to strike the audacious blows by which he weakened the House of Austria and raised Prussia, with her five million inhabitants, to the rank of a first-rate power.

Charles VI left no male heir to the Austrian lands, but he managed to secure from all the courts of Europe a guarantee that his daughter Maria Theresa should succeed to the Hapsburg claims. But Frederick, ignoring the Pragmatic Sanction to which Prussia had been a signatory, invited France and Bavaria to join him in seizing the lands of the young and inexperienced Empress-Queen. For his own share Frederick coveted the province of Silesia; having secured it by a swift campaign, he made peace with Maria Theresa at Breslau in 1742. Then, fearing that Austria might recover too rapidly from her misfortunes, he rejoined France and Bavaria in the field, only to desert them a second time by the Peace of Dresden in 1745. "Happy are they," he wrote after extricating himself with his spoils for the second time, "who, having secured their own safety, can tranquilly regard the embarrassment of others."

• *Civil Reforms*   The reestablishment of peace between Prussia and Austria in 1745 left Frederick free to turn his restless mind to problems of civil administration. Rising before six in the morning, he spent the hours of the forenoon laboring over the business of state. No department of government escaped his scrutiny and no detail appeared too petty for his attention. While still in his early thirties he had proved himself one of the most brilliant generals of the age; he was now to win equal fame as an exponent of the form of government which is known as enlightened despotism. The most influential writings of the *philosophes* on this subject did not appear until after 1750, but before that date Frederick had recognized many of the abuses they were later to attack and had anticipated the remedies they recommended for them. While his services in organizing the administration of the Prussian state cannot here be discussed at length, the present account would be incomplete without at least a short summary of his reforms. The manner in which Frederick used the military resources *Military* of Prussia in the War of the Austrian Succession demonstrated his energy, ruthlessness, power of decision, and skill in choosing competent subordinates. These qualities served him equally well in civil administration. Even in peacetime he ran his kingdom with the severity of a military barracks. He made frequent unannounced inspections, had his officials report on one another, and punished laziness, disobedience, and dishonesty with severe penalties. As "first servant of the state" he set an example of tireless industry, devotion to duty, simplicity in food and dress, and frugality in expenditure.

The center of Frederick's government was the royal council, but his ministers had little independent authority and he treated them with brusqueness and sometimes with contempt. Dispatches, petitions, and reports from all parts of his domains poured in daily, and he spent his mornings going through them and scribbling or dictating comments and replies. His unwillingness to delegate authority limited the initiative of his officials, and his impatience, arrogance, and sarcasm often cut him off from sage advice. His administrative departments were never systematically coordinated; he set up new ministries—for the army, for Silesia, for trade and industry— when he wished to push through important reforms. Under a ruler of energy and genius these administrative methods worked reasonably well, but rulers of energy and genius are rare. This is one of the most serious defects of hereditary monarchy as a system of government, and Frederick had no remedy for it.

• *Economic Policies* One weakness—the threat of insolvency —Frederick did manage to avoid with skill and resolution. His economies affected all areas of his administration and he insisted that state revenues must exceed expenditures. He tried to make the taxes levied on his subjects proportionate to their income. In a *Political Testament*, which he wrote as a guide, he declared that "Taxation should not affect the worker, the soldier, or the impoverished, but only the well-to-do and the rich." Despite such humane maxims, however, all classes felt the burden of the levies and excise duties which he imposed, but the burden was not excessive. Some of the most unpopular imposts were those he levied on wine and coffee which he discouraged his subjects from drinking because they had to be imported.

Agriculture and industry benefited from Frederick's constant attention despite his occasional misjudgments and arbitrary decrees. Farmers were encouraged to cultivate potatoes and sugar beets, to plant clover and turnips for fodder, and to reclaim wastelands and marshes. Immigrants attracted from other countries were settled in sparsely peopled areas and given tools and animals to begin their new life. Sheep's wool could not be exported under penalty of death until it had been woven into cloth. Silk, on the other hand, which it proved difficult to produce in northern Europe, was imported raw and exported as fabric.

Frederick was a mercantilist in his economic policies: he sought to restrict imports and increase exports. He took pains to encourage the manufacture of porcelain, leather goods, and wool, silk, and cotton textiles. He stimulated trade within his domains by constructing better roads and canals and reducing tax barriers to internal commerce. Purchase of cloth, shoes, and weapons for the army provided a large and steady market for standardized goods—"Armies supplied the first great markets for mass consumption in modern times."[1] As the Prussian armed forces, even in peacetime, required four-fifths of the state revenues for their support, this military outlay played a vital part in the Prussian economy by assuring a constant market for the products of farm and factory.

• *Legal and Educational Reforms* In his plans to reform the laws and improve the administration of justice, Frederick consulted Samuel von Cocceji, a jurist who had been appointed Chief Justice of Prussia by Frederick William I. Cocceji hoped to reduce the laws in force throughout Prussia to a single consistent code and to raise the standards of court personnel and procedure. These aims were largely realized during Frederick's

[1] Walter L. Dorn, *Competition for Empire, 1740–1763*, (New York, 1940) p. 15.

reign (1740–1786), although the code of law for the whole kingdom did not go into effect until 1795. By modern standards Prussian law remained severe, but Frederick eased some of the crueler punishments—for example he abolished the death penalty for abortion. Also, from time to time, he overruled his justices and mitigated their sentences. In the case of a blasphemer who had been condemned for cursing God, the king, and the judge, Frederick observed with wry humor, "That he blasphemed against God proved he does not know Him; for his slander of me I forgive him; but to insult a noble Counsellor calls for exemplary punishment: imprison him for half-an-hour."

A program to improve the schools, likewise introduced under Frederick William I, was carried forward more vigorously under his son's direction. Children from five to thirteen were ordered to attend their local school and parents could be fined if they failed to send them there. Royal instructions covered all the details of school methods and administration from the textbooks to the teachers' salaries. Furthermore, in an age when education was still largely controlled by the clergy, Frederick insisted that "all schools and universities are state institutions" and he specified that they should be open to state inspection at all times.

• *The Prussian Army* "You alone must supervise the revenue and keep the command of the army resolutely in your hands." So Frederick William I admonished his son in his final instructions, and Frederick the Great lived up to the advice. The Prussian army remained to the close of his life the instrument in which Frederick reposed his chief trust for the safety of his state. From 80,000 he increased it during his reign to nearly 200,000 men; he wrote treatises on the science of warfare for the instruction of his generals; and his death was hastened by a chill contracted during a military review. To understand the faith which he placed in a well-disciplined army, a faith which he had found to be justified, it is necessary to turn to the events of the Seven Years' War when the courage of the Prussian soldiers and the skill of their king were all that saved Prussia from being divided among the neighboring powers.

• *The Seven Years' War* The empire of the Hapsburgs, like a falling house that never falls, had surprised its enemies by weathering all adversities, and when the War of the Austrian Succession ended in 1748 Maria Theresa had won back all her hereditary dominions except Silesia. Frederick watched the recovery of Austria with apprehension. He knew that Maria Theresa would never forget Silesia and that he might have to fight again to retain the province which he had snatched, for the duel between Hapsburgs and Hohenzollerns for leadership in the German lands had barely commenced. During the eight years of peace that followed, from 1748 to 1756, while Frederick was reorganizing the Prussian state, Maria Theresa likewise attempted to introduce a greater degree of centralization and efficiency into the administration of the Hapsburg domains. As Archduchess of Austria, and Queen of Bohemia and Hungary, she ruled an empire possessed of five times the resources of Prussia.[1] She refused to regard Silesia as irretrievably lost.

Throughout its history the House of Austria had been weakened by the fact that the Hapsburg possessions could never be forged into a national state. The subjects of Maria Theresa spoke ten different languages and represented as

[1] Maria Theresa's titles and the manner in which she acquired them puzzle many students. Her father, Charles VI, wished to leave her his undivided inheritance, but a woman could not properly be Emperor of the Holy Roman Empire nor King of Hungary. On his death, Maria Theresa became Archduchess of Austria and Queen of Bohemia, but the Hungarian diet bargained before accepting her as "King" of Hungary. The war of the Austrian Succession cost her Silesia, and the duchies of Parma and Piacenza and part of the Duchy of Milan, in Italy; but her husband, the modest Francis Stephen, who had become grand duke of Tuscany in 1737, brought that Italian domain into the Hapsburg inheritance, and he was elected Emperor of the Holy Roman Empire in 1745. Maria Theresa, as his wife, thus became an empress and is usually referred to as the Empress Maria Theresa. She was not, however, empress *of Austria*. The title Emperor of Austria was first used by her grandson Francis I in 1804.

many nationalities; however deep their loyalty to the Empress-Queen, they felt no common Austrian patriotism. Furthermore, the various provinces possessed local privileges which rendered the centralization of power in the hands of the monarch a difficult policy to pursue. Maria Theresa was careful to respect the prejudices of her subjects; cautious and diplomatic by nature, she feared to attempt a reconstruction of the government from its foundations. Her reforms, in their incompleteness, have been aptly compared to the addition of modern wings to a feudal castle.

These circumstances made it impossible for Austria to rival the bureaucratic efficiency of the Prussian state, but Maria Theresa proved more fortunate than Frederick in securing allies. Frederick's audacious ambition to build up a third power capable of exercising an equal share with the Bourbons and Hapsburgs in the management of European affairs drove those rival dynasties together. In 1756 Austria and France forgot an enmity dating from the fifteenth century and signed a treaty of alliance at Versailles; but although Maria Theresa gained one ally she lost another. In the War of the Austrian Succession she had enjoyed the benefit of English aid, but Great Britain was engaged in a colonial struggle with France and could not be expected to support Austria in her new course. Consequently, while from 1740 to 1748 Austria and England had fought Prussia and France, from 1756 to 1763 Austria and France were to fight Prussia and England. The change in Austrian policy which brought about this new alignment of the Great Powers is known as the Diplomatic Revolution.

With France won over to the Austrian side, a result largely due to Maria Theresa's skilful minister, Count Kaunitz, the coalition against Frederick seemed complete. Austria, Russia, France, Saxony, and Sweden, acting together, could hardly fail to crush any resistance Frederick might offer; the allies foresaw an easy victory, to be followed by the dismemberment of the Prussian kingdom. As the plot matured Frederick learned through secret channels of the fate that was being prepared for him. In 1756 he came to an agreement with the only possible ally that remained, and signed the Convention of Westminster with Great Britain; then, rather than wait until the Russians, Austrians, and French were ready to attack him, he forced them into the field prematurely by a sudden descent upon Saxony, seized the resources of that state, and compelled its army to swear allegiance to himself. To the Saxon commander's protest that history afforded no precedent for such an act, Frederick responded that he prided himself upon being somewhat original.

In the seven years that followed, this young prince, whom his father had once planned to disinherit, proved himself the most brilliant general of his age, and baffled his opponents by a defense among the most desperate and successful that history describes. In 1761 Great Britain withdrew her subsidies; and in the succeeding year, when the game must have grown too desperate to last, Frederick was saved by the death of his implacable enemy, the Czarina Elizabeth of Russia. Her successor, Peter III, was a warm admirer of the Prussian king; he not only deserted the coalition, but sent a Russian detachment to Frederick's support. With the turn of the tide the French court, weary of the struggle, made a separate peace, and Maria Theresa, forsaken by both her allies, was forced to acquiesce a third time in the loss of Silesia. The Treaty of Hubertsburg, concluded in February, 1763, re-established the *status quo ante* between Austria and Prussia in every particular.

JOSEPH II

• *Youth and Education of Joseph*, 1741–1765 Until her death in 1780 Maria Theresa kept the affairs of government in her own hands. Her epitaph read: *Sexu femina, ingenio vir* (In sex a woman, in abilities a man). Joseph had to wait until his fortieth year to enjoy the undivided authority he desired. The reforms he had meditated but had been unable to apply absorbed his thoughts, and the delay made him impatient of restraints upon his authority and impetuous in the use of it. These circumstances help to explain his character as a ruler and the frustrations of his reign.

As Maria Theresa gave birth to sixteen children, while devoting herself to her subjects' welfare, it is not surprising that her sons and daughters lacked a thorough education. Joseph showed some talent for music, but no deep appreciation for art or literature, and he received little real grounding in the exact sciences. For the problems of statecraft, however, he manifested a lively interest. His most eminent instructor in the science of government was Karl Anton Martini, a disciple of the German philosopher Wolff, and a leader of the Enlightenment in the Austrian lands. Martini's writings indicate that he was a convert to the theory of natural law in its most dogmatic form. That Joseph was influenced by his views and accepted them with favor may be surmised from the honors he later conferred upon his tutor, but it would be a mistake to attribute to any one source ideas which were the property of all enlightened thinkers in that age. Joseph might have found similar doctrines in any work of the *philosophes* which he studied.

• *Joseph As Co-regent*, 1765–1780 In Maria Theresa's nature the heart of a woman was joined to the mind and spirit of a king; though not the equal of a Catharine or an Elizabeth, she must be ranked among the great queens of history. A sovereign in her own right, she refused to share her authority; despite the extravagant love she felt for Francis of Lorraine, she early recognized his incompetence, and never allowed him more than a shadow of the imperial dignity. When he died in 1765 Joseph had already been chosen to succeed him as Holy Roman Emperor, but again the title was to carry little power. Though appointed co-regent with his mother, Joseph obtained no share in the management of internal affairs. He was allowed to interest himself in the reorganization of the army, and in foreign politics; but his freedom of action was so carefully circumscribed that on two occasions he begged to resign his dignities unless he could enjoy the measure of authority which should by right pertain to them. The conflict between mother and son became at times so bitter that Maria Theresa spoke of retiring to a nunnery; but in the end, Joseph, who was a dutiful son, always yielded, accepting as gracefully as he could his ineffective role.

The secret of his frustration lay as much in his own character as in his mother's opposition. It is the fate of princes to have few real friends, but had Joseph possessed the personality for it he might have headed a party of reform, or forced his way into the government by some other method. Unfortunately his nature was cold and unmagnetic, and he failed to create confidence or attract a following. Though Joseph could assume at will an air of candor and informality, Frederick the Great detected at their first meeting that his frankness was simulated. Nor did Joseph's inadequate education escape the sharp judgment of the Prussian king. "With all his desire to acquire knowledge," the latter wrote, "he lacks the patience to teach himself." Yet Frederick did not despise, nor altogether dislike this "Caesar possessed by demons." Perhaps he recollected the craving for glory and the impatience of restraint which had tormented him in his own youth.

Frederick had been given a chance to gratify his ambitious nature by conquering Silesia at twenty-nine; but Joseph, as he passed into his thirties and found his schemes as far as ever from realization, developed a stubborn and bitter sense of frustration. No doubt of himself or of his methods troubled him, but he became more and more exasperated with the stupidity of others. Much as he had studied the character of Frederick, that monarch's greatest quality had escaped him. Frederick, as Carlyle has said, was a Reality. He possessed the clarity of vision of a genius; he judged himself with the same cynical realism that he applied to others, and was the first to admit his own failures and mistakes. To Joseph such impersonal analysis was impossible. He was a poor judge of men; he had mediocre talents and the mind of a doctrinaire; his one approach to genius was his infinite capacity for taking pains.

Few rulers have worked more conscientiously. He plagued his mother with unsolicited projects for the abolition of serfdom, the suppression of the monasteries, the proclamation of religious toleration. But Maria Theresa would not disrupt the social order unduly, and Joseph's anticlerical sentiments shocked her orthodoxy. In her own cautious manner she had introduced many reforms—in education, in agriculture, in finance, and in the Church. The Inquisition was suppressed in Milan; the use of torture was restricted; the Jesuits were expelled from the Hapsburg domains. Such concessions to the spirit of the Enlightenment Joseph regarded as palliative measures, little better than useless so long as the basic principles of government went unreformed. He wrote his brother Leopold in 1772:

> The work piles up daily, and nothing is done. I labor unceasingly all morning, and until five and six in the afternoon, with fifteen minutes out while I eat a solitary lunch, but there is no result. The petty objections, the intrigues of which I have so long been the victim, hinder and obstruct me, and with the delay everything is going to the devil.

• *First Partition of Poland,* 1772   So Joseph turned his attention to foreign affairs. Out of admiration for Frederick he urged an alliance with Prussia, and Maria Theresa was at last persuaded to let him visit that kingdom. In 1769 Catharine of Russia was pressing a victorious campaign against the Turks which filled the Viennese court with alarm; it was hoped that Austria and Prussia, if united, might check the Muscovite ambitions. Joseph met the great enemy of his House at Neisse and succumbed at once to the fascination of Frederick's personality. "We talked," he wrote his mother, "of legislation, of Voltaire, of a hundred things which it is impossible to recount." A sense of caution, it may be, kept him from being more explicit; he was aware of the disapproval with which Maria Theresa regarded the king of Prussia's unorthodox opinions. "I hear," Voltaire wrote Frederick, "that you have been initiating the Emperor into our holy mysteries."

As a diplomat Joseph proved himself naïve and not very successful. The following year a second interview was arranged between the two monarchs, but this time it was the Austrian minister Kaunitz who negotiated the agreement. War between Austria and Russia over the Turkish question appeared all but unavoidable. Frederick, who had friendly understandings with both states, labored to avert hostilities, and the dispute was finally settled by all three powers agreeing to seek com-

pensation by annexing a portion of Poland. The result was a
race between Austrian, Prussian, and Russian troops to oc-
cupy coveted sections of that defenseless country; and this
First Partition of Poland, as it is termed, was ratified by a
treaty signed at St. Petersburg in 1772.

• *The Potato War* (1778–1779) It has already been pointed
out how Austria and France, by a readjustment of alliances
known as the Diplomatic Revolution, relaxed their ancient
rivalry and joined in a compact for mutual defense in 1756.
That this agreement outlasted the Seven Years' War must be
credited to the endeavours of the Austrian minister Kaunitz,
for it was unpopular in both Paris and Vienna. Joseph, in
particular, was hostile towards the French Court; and Louis
XVI (1774-1792), though he had married the Emperor's sister
Marie Antoinette, distrusted and disliked his brother-in-law.
Fear of the Russians, however, held Austria from breaking
with France, and in 1777 Joseph was dispatched to Paris in
an attempt to establish the alliance on a firmer foundation.
As a diplomatic overture the visit was a failure; it served
merely to disgust Joseph with Parisian frivolity and to convince him more strongly than ever of the worthlessness of the
agreement.

The House of Austria derived in truth little real advantage
from an alliance with the Bourbons; the Court of Versailles,
while collaborating in minor matters, blocked every important
Hapsburg ambition; and the Emperor had barely ended his
stay in Paris when a crisis taught him unmistakably the
hollowness of French friendship. In December 1777, the Elector
of Bavaria died without male issue, and Joseph, imitating
Frederick's Silesian *coup*, immediately laid claim to and
occupied a third of the Bavarian domains. Ever vigilant to resist Hapsburg aggression, Frederick protested vigorously. As
the diplomatic argument grew tense both Austria and Prussia
dispatched large armies into the field; for Joseph, while pro-
testing his desire for peace, burned with secret ambition to
try his skill against the greatest general of the age. But Maria

Theresa would not support his warlike attitude. Without his knowledge she wrote to Frederick begging him to avert bloodshed, and to Catharine the Great invoking Russian mediation. France, the ally of Austria, renounced her treaty obligations and refused the stipulated aid. Swift to gauge the change in the currents and finding Joseph's army well intrenched, Frederick preferred to win his point by diplomacy. The campaign from which Joseph had planned to gain renown passed off without a battle, and because of the activity of the troops in hunting forage was ridiculed by contemporaries as the Potato War. By the terms of peace signed at Teschen in May 1779, Austria was compelled to withdraw from all but a fraction of the disputed territory.

• *Joseph as Sole Ruler,* 1780–1790   When Maria Theresa's death ended her forty-year reign in 1780, Joseph held at last the undivided authority he craved and the opportunity to apply his long-meditated reforms. He did not realize how serious the obstacles would prove, nor could he foresee that he had only ten more years to live.

Behind Joseph's zeal for reform lay a humanitarian concern for the happiness of his subjects. Governments existed, it seemed clear to him, in order that they might safeguard the welfare of the people. His political researches had convinced him that the most efficient form of government was a highly organized machine which could absorb into a central bureaucracy the details of local administration, and establish throughout the realm a rigid uniformity of language, law, and custom. To introduce simplicity and standardization into the chaotic administration of the Hapsburg dominions appeared to him the evident duty of an enlightened despot; but behind this humanistic zeal lay an unacknowledged motive, a desire to make himself master of an aggressive, centralized, military state.

• *Financial Reforms*   Physiocratic doctrines had exercised too strong a sway over Joseph's thinking for him to doubt that sound finances were the bases of efficient government. As co-regent he had labored to balance the Austrian budget, sub-scribing part of his personal fortune to achieve the desired re-sult; but at his accession an accurate estimate of the revenue and expenditure of the state was still unobtainable. The prob-lem of accumulating capital, of enriching himself and his peo-ple, claimed his closest attention. He lived simply, almost fru-gally, indifferent to the charges of miserliness which his econ-omies brought him. "Saving and scrimping," jeered Frederick, "saving and scrimping, that is all he sets his heart upon."

The Emperor's passion for fiscal experiments excited little enthusiasm among his subjects: parsimony is an unprincely virtue. Furthermore, his attempts to make each taxpayer a di-rect contributor to the royal exchequer struck too definitely at the feudal system to escape bitter opposition; and the scheme for protective tariffs which he introduced pleased only a few manufacturers. "In financial matters," he wrote Leopold of Tuscany, "I cannot find a soul who understands me or has a single idea of the elements of the thing. In all honor, I do not know how I am going to manage."

Yet he held himself stubbornly to the task until the years of soul-devouring toil had their reward. In 1786 the Austrian budget showed a revenue of 88 million gulden against an ex-penditure of 85 million. It was a fleeting triumph. The follow-ing year witnessed the outbreak of a ruinous war with Turkey, and Joseph's last months were clouded by the knowledge that despite all his expedients he must leave to his successor a na-tional debt which extended at the time of his death to 400 million gulden.

● *Religious Reforms* As a child of the Enlightenment, Jo-seph favored a wide tolerance in religious affairs. He was no freethinker; to the end of his life he remained a circumspect if not an ardent communicant of the Roman Catholic Church; but like Frederick the Great he felt that his subjects might safely be left to seek the road to heaven after their own fashion. One of the first edicts which followed his accession proclaimed the equality of non-Catholics before the law. Permission was ac-corded members of the heretical sects to hold civil or military office, to erect churches of their own, to establish schools and seminaries. Even the Jews were allowed to lay aside the peculiar costume which had been for centuries the symbol of their humiliating status.

As a further step Joseph decided to disestablish the monasteries. Their wealth was a source of annoyance to him; it irked his economic soul that gold should lie idle when it might be circulating to the common good. He disliked moreover to have in his dominions brotherhoods, the members of which stood outside the jurisdiction of the civil courts, and looked to Rome for their instructions. Successive decrees limited the number of monks and nuns that might be admitted to the cloister; a pension was provided for members of the disestablished orders; and monks so desiring were encouraged to take up secular occupations. Leopold of Tuscany observed with interest the progress of these hardy measures, but he declined to keep pace with them. "In Italy," he explained to Joseph, "the people are much more deeply attached to the brotherhoods than in Germany." Perhaps, with the tact characteristic of him, he wished to sound a note of caution, but if so the warning passed unheeded.

Even the ritual of the Church did not escape Joseph's attention. A contempt for ceremonial display was one of his strongest characteristics, and this, combined with the impatience of the rationalist at a complicated liturgy, led him to attempt a simplification of the Church services. For the money commonly lavished upon gilded images and superfluous pageantry he found more practical uses, and the same desire for economy moved him to forbid all processions and pilgrimages. At the same time fifteen Saints' Days were stricken from the calendar on the ground that they afforded the people too many holidays. Work was more important than worship.

Papal protests at this rough treatment of the Church proving of no avail, Pope Pius VI decided in 1782 to visit Vienna in person. Unable to dissuade the Holy Father from his purpose, Joseph prepared to welcome him with every show of respect; but he refused to moderate his anti-clerical measures in any particular. The rationalists of Europe enjoyed the spectacle of papal impotence and affected to marvel at the courtesy and forbearance with which Joseph treated his uninvited guest. "I do not envy Your Majesty the rare privilege of being lodged face to face with Pius VI," wrote Catharine. "... A priest like that is a somewhat incommodious piece of furniture." Joseph's reply echoed the same note of irreverence. "The interest, may I venture to say the friendliness, with which Her Majesty has written regarding the Italian priest who recently oppressed me with his visit warms me with gratitude. ... The Pope gained nothing of importance; but I managed to treat him in such a manner as to avoid a definite rupture."

• *Juristic Reforms* Of the confusion which distinguished the administration of justice under the old regime, the overlapping jurisdictions, the conflicting codes, the arbitrary arrests and inhuman punishments, no adequate picture can be attempted here. Within the confines of a single province the same offence might involve penalties which ranged from a light fine to mutilation or death; yet as the *philosophes* never tired of pointing out, it was impossible that there could be two punishments for the same crime and both of them just. The voice of reason and of humanity urged the suppression of the many courts and codes, and the establishment in their place of a uniform system of civil and criminal law applicable in every instance.

In the Austrian lands justice was confused by a mass of customs, charters, feudal privileges, papal proclamations, and imperial edicts, which formed a legal tangle past all unraveling. Maria Theresa appointed a commission of lawyers in 1753 to codify the existing legislation; after fourteen years it published eight volumes of decrees, but the work was less a code than a collection. A compilation of the criminal laws, the *Nemesis Theresiana*, was published in 1768; but this likewise bore that stamp of incompleteness which impaired the value of almost all Maria Theresa's reforms.

As Joseph envisaged it the administration of justice was a simple function of the state, his idea of legal reform being to solve all disputes by establishing throughout the Empire the single jurisdiction of the imperial courts. A supreme council at Vienna, appellate courts in the larger cities, and magistracies for each town, were the elements of his plan; but since he could not shatter to bits the sorry scheme of things as he found it, the problem of remolding it proved beyond his skill. Concessions and compromises soon blotted the bold outlines of his project; thick-headed subordinates completed the confusion. His new codes pleased no one: jurists in the Netherlands fought the abolition of torture; humanists in Vienna condemned the new scale of punishments as merciless; the privileged classes everywhere stood aghast at a decree which established civil equality before the law. In the presence of a universal and insistent clamor of disapproval Joseph hardened his heart.

• *Administrative Reforms* Familiar from his youth with the exercise of military authority, the new Emperor had carried into the affairs of civil administration an inflexibility of temper reminiscent of barrack-room discipline. An empire, he felt, like an army, required a centralized command; he would have agreed with Du Pont de Nemours that the idea of several authorities in the same state was an absurdity. The triumph of his ideals required the destruction of the feudal courts, of the provincial estates, the monastic orders, in fact of all autonomous groups in the empire, and the substitution of an imperial bureaucracy in which the Church, the army, the judiciary, were each to be a department of government officered by civil servants.

A beginning had been made in this direction by the creation of a Council of State at Vienna in 1761. By appointing a hierarchy of royal officials and shifting to them the authority previously vested in the nobles, the national monarchs of Europe had found a way to humble their feudal dependents. It was a policy which Louis XIV of France had pursued with particular success, and Joseph planned to follow it unswervingly in the Hapsburg lands. When the suppression of the provincial estates and the curtailment of local liberties alarmed his Belgian and Hungarian subjects and finally goaded them into revolution he was at a loss to understand their opposition to measures so clearly salutary. "I leave you to judge the extent of my despair," he wrote Leopold. "I am the only one holding to the true course, and I am left to labor it alone. The Council of State avails as little as if it had never existed. I am without any assistance whatsoever. Dispatches, replies, everything is left for me to attend to." Joseph was reaping the difficulties of solitary despotism.

• *Educational Reforms* All the leaders of the Enlightenment attached great importance to the problem of education; a child rationally reared, it seemed to them, could not fail to become an intelligent and virtuous citizen. Public instruction had been neglected in the past; but it was too important a function to be resigned indefinitely to village schoolmasters, or left in the hands of the Church. In this field, as in all others, Joseph entertained enlightened but dogmatic views. He proposed to amalgamate the Austrian universities, together with the intermediate and primary schools, into a single system and to administer them as a department of government. A revised curriculum and state-salaried teachers were to grind out a steady stream of efficient civil servants; the schools would become factories, machines for making more machines.

Nor would maturity bring to the citizens an escape from state tutelage. Frederick the Great once boasted that he and his subjects had an unofficial bargain: he was to do as he liked and they might say what they pleased; but the Austrian peoples under Joseph II could pretend to no such privilege. A paternal government treated them as children, and their manners and morals were made the object of a constant and irritating supervision. Although at the opening of his reign Joseph relaxed the censorship, he later made it more stringent; foreign periodicals were excluded from the Hapsburg dominions; and large rewards were posted for the apprehension of unauthorized pamphleteers. Petitions on behalf of freedom of speech or of the press left Joseph unmoved. "The father of a family," he said, "who holds the welfare of his children at heart must not allow himself to be turned from a salutary course because of ill-judged complaints."

• *Social Reforms* Since of all classes in the state the serfs alone had nothing to lose they could afford to view without alarm the headstrong course of the reforming emperor. Indeed, long after his death stories of his simplicity, his accessibility, his democratic tastes were preserved among the peasants whose welfare he had striven to promote. For the noble orders Joseph had little use; to a distrust born of political exigencies he added a dislike that was purely personal; and his humane decrees for the liberation of the serfs neglected to provide adequate compensation for the masters. Hence, not unnaturally, the nobles showed no noticeable enthusiasm for the success of the Emperor's measures: the liberated serfs were left to shift for themselves; some prospered, but others proved unequal to the responsibilities of their new estate. The blame for these difficulties of adjustment the Emperor, as always, attributed to the malice and stupidity of others. "I lack servants of every sort," he complained, "either for planning or for executing my designs. To be frank, I have found scarcely one person who is filled with a genuine zeal for the good of the country."

Joseph never learned to suffer fools gladly. "The Emperor," laments the diary of a councilor, "acts as if . . . he alone loved the country and knew what was right, and all his subordinates were either rascals or blockheads." The letters to Leopold of Tuscany tell the same story. "No one here has assimilated the rules I laid down," concludes one exasperated passage. "The heads of the civil service still follow their old ruts, signing without a glance at the contents any paper that is set before them." And again, "This business of repeating the same thing week after week is killing me." Yet even in his blackest moods a sense of duty held him to his task. "I have been slaving away in my study," he confesses in one place, "seeking some means to organize and simplify my work a little; but laboring against so many obstacles has reduced me to such a pitch of hopelessness that were my heart not set upon the thing I would have to give up in despair."

• *The Reopening of the Scheldt*   By the Peace of Westphalia (1648) which ended the Thirty Years' War the river Scheldt was closed to all save Dutch ships, and a line of barrier fortresses erected in the Spanish Netherlands to protect the frontier between France and Holland. When the Spanish Netherlands passed to the House of Austria by the Treaty of Utrecht (1713) these terms remained in force; for by closing the Scheldt the merchants of Amsterdam had been able to cut off the sea-trade of Antwerp, and to profit by their rival's decline.

Joseph II began his reign with the intention already formed of abolishing this restriction upon the trade of his Belgian provinces. In 1782, finding Holland at war with Great Britain, he seized the opportunity to repudiate the convention closing the Scheldt, at the same time dismantling the barrier fortresses in an endeavor to conciliate France. As usual his calculations miscarried. The first ship which he dispatched to Antwerp was fired upon by the Dutch; French assistance, upon which he had built high hopes, failed to materialize; Russia was secretly hostile. Baffled, Joseph consented after long quibbling to renounce his project; but to cover his defeat he demanded from the Dutch an indemnity of 10 million gulden. Relieved to see the matter settled, the powers assisted him to collect it. *Trinkgeld* (a tip) was Frederick's contemptuous epithet for the transaction.

• *The Bavarian Question Again*   The ill-success which thus attended his aggressive policy in the Low Countries may have helped to turn Joseph's mind back to another project of his, the exchange of his Belgian provinces for Bavaria. By the Peace of Teschen, which closed the Potato War in 1779, the House of Austria had renounced all further claims upon the electorate, but even if Joseph had possessed a tender conscience about such promises (which was far from being the case) the thought of rounding out his empire by the addition of a wealthy dukedom might well have subdued his scruples. Lying between Bohemia and the Rhine, Bavaria seemed naturally fitted to become a cornerstone of the Austrian Empire, and to assure for all time the predominance of the Hapsburgs in German affairs.

To Charles Theodore, the reigning elector, Joseph offered in

1784 the title of King of Burgundy, with Brussels for his capital, if he would hand over Bavaria to the Imperial Crown. Few transactions, even in that age of cynical diplomacy, showed a more complete disregard for the wishes of the subject peoples; Bavaria and the Austrian Netherlands were to be bought and sold like country estates. For the House of Austria the exchange promised striking advantages; the Belgian provinces were alien and inaccessible, while Bavaria, with a population of nearly three million German Catholics, could be assimilated into the empire and would protect the northern frontier. Joseph pressed on the negotiations with zeal.

From his retreat at *Sans Souci* the aging Frederick watched the plot mature. Charles Theodore, it was evident, had sold himself to Austria; but his heir, the Duke of Zweibrücken, had still to be consulted, and might be persuaded, by judicious hints, to oppose the Hapsburg schemes. In January 1785, Joseph's projects met with sudden disaster. The Duke of Zweibrücken protested against the negotiations and appealed to Frederick for justice; and the people of Bavaria, learning with indignation of the fate proposed for them, so frightened Charles Theodore that he denied all knowledge of the proposed exchange. At *Sans Souci* Frederick accepted the compliments of ambassadors on his unselfish solicitude for the rights of the Bavarians. He suggested the formation of a league of German princes to put a stop to Joseph's aggressions. It amused the conqueror of Silesia to pose as a champion of order and legitimacy.

• *The Road to Byzantium* The alliance between Austria and Russia born of Joseph's visit to St. Petersburg in 1780 had as its object the aggrandizement of both powers at the expense of Turkey. How the spoils of conquest were to be divided had been left for the moment unsettled; but both Joseph and Catharine had visions of entering Constantinople in triumph and reviving the ancient glories of Byzantium. Their alliance was thus an unnatural one, and any success won by either power was certain to strain their friendly understanding. In the nineteenth

century the continued decline of Turkey sharpened the eagerness of both Austria and Russia to outwit the other in winning
the Turkish heritage, and their intrigues created the problem
known in diplomatic history as the Near Eastern Question.

Until it fell into the hands of the Turks in 1453,
Constantinople had been the capital of the Eastern Roman
Empire. As successor of Charlemagne, Joseph dreamed of
making it once again acknowledge the sway of an Emperor
Ever August of the Romans. In December 1787, partly in the
hope of taking the Turks by surprise, partly to anticipate
Catharine, he launched an army of 200 thousand men against
Belgrade. This discreditable maneuver (there had been no
declaration of war) failed in its objective; the campaign of 1788
turned against the Austrians, and Joseph's army, attacked on
the flank, was forced into a disastrous retreat. Catharine made
no real effort to relieve her ally; she had intended from the
first to let Joseph draw upon himself the malignance of the
Turks and the disapproval of Europe. Protected from invasion
herself by the wide Russian steppes, she watched the Austrian
cordons writhe and struggle in their vain efforts to save the
smiling valleys of the Banat from the fury of the Ottoman
hordes.

The morbid mind of the Emperor led him to exaggerate a reverse into a catastrophe; in desperation he cashiered general
after general as responsible for a disaster which he himself had
invited. "Nothing more terrible, more piteous, more shameful,
could have happened," he wrote Leopold. "My plans have all
been destroyed by those who should have forwarded them.
I demand of you whether I am not the most wretched being
alive, enduring the utmost that it is possible to bear of moral
and physical suffering?" Mental distress, added to the hard-
ships of the campaign, had broken his health; but unable to
accept the fact of his own incompetence he refused to resign
the command of the army. "I would rather die under a tree,"
he protested, "than abandon things in their present state, for
the Marshall is so discouraged himself that he no longer knows
what to do." He held out until December, when the troops

had somewhat recovered their morale. Then, so weak that he could scarcely ride a horse, he returned to Vienna.

• *The Last Phase* The program of internal reforms, entrusted to subordinates during Joseph's absence in the field, had become involved in a more hopeless confusion than ever. With the concentration of troops in the South the Austrian Netherlands were left free to assert their independence, and they took prompt advantage of this opportunity. This revolt of Joseph's Belgian subjects is exceptional enough to deserve notice, for it was inspired not by a desire for reforms but by opposition to them. His cancellation of established privileges and substitution of nine governors and a central council in place of the complex institutions under which the provinces had been ruled since the Middle Ages angered the Belgians to the point of revolution. The hatred of Austria thus fostered led them two years later to welcome the French revolutionary armies, and to accept willingly in the name of liberty reforms more drastic than those Joseph had introduced in the name of efficiency. Few examples could illustrate better the hatred which Joseph was capable of inspring, or prove more clearly the innate weakness of enlightened despotism as a method of reform.

The Belgian revolution was not the only problem that faced Joseph when he returned to Vienna at the close of 1788. A revolt was likewise threatening among the natives of the Tyrol; and the nobles of Hungary were on the point of throwing off their allegiance to the House of Hapsburg. With that close application which had become a habit with him the Emperor sought to study the causes of the general discontent. He studied dispatches, questioned officials, and called for the minutes of the various councils. But his old power of concentration had gone; the slightest effort or excitement set his pulse racing; his head ached interminably.

Thoughts of the work that was piling up pursued him, crowding all relaxation from his days and filling the nights with disquietude. Ten years of failure had passed since he

talked so confidently of reform with Frederick at Neisse, and
the Prussian King warned him against that slavery to details
which is a vexation to the spirit, blinding it to the larger
things of life. Now Frederick was dead and Joseph was dying.
"I am distressed that your cough should prove so persistent,"
Leopold had written more than once. In April 1789, came the
first hemorrhage. "The ailment which has been tormenting
me these nine months," he wrote Leopold, "suddenly resulted
in a vomiting of blood. . . .They applied leeches, but I still
continued to cough up blood, more in fact than ever. . . ."
Leeches for a pulmonary hemorrhage!

His last months Joseph passed in solitude, almost unat-
tended. "I am unable to leave my room," he wrote in December.
"I receive no one, for it is difficult to sustain a conversation,
and I am left alone with my problems and my thoughts which
are not happy ones." Kaunitz refused outright to visit the
emperor's sickroom; lesser functionaries became evasive or un-
manageable. Slowly the conviction established itself in Joseph's
mind that his officials either would not or could not execute
his commands, and the consciousness of failure obsessed him.
"Here lies Joseph II," ran his self-chosen epitaph, "who was
unfortunate in everything that he undertook." On January
30, 1790, he withdrew most of his reforms; the task of tran-
quilizing the distracted empire was his bequest to the more
tactful Leopold. He died the 20th of February, a man, in the
words of Lord Bryce, "than whom few have more narrowly
missed greatness."

CATHARINE THE GREAT

• *Russia before Catharine's Accession* Until the eighteenth
century Russia had little direct influence on European affairs.
The reign of Peter the Great (1689–1725), who admired
European civilization and aspired to transform his backward
realm by introducing western methods and techniques, marked
a turning point in Russian history. Peter opened "windows
to the West" by pushing the Russian frontier westward to

the shores of the Baltic Sea, and in the end he founded a new Russian capital, St. Petersburg (now Leningrad), at the head of the Gulf of Finland. The pursuit of this purpose, however, involved him in a long war with Sweden and its warrior-king Charles XII.

It is interesting to recall that the eighteenth century in Europe opened with two simultaneous and exhausting wars, both caused by the territorial ambitions of despotic rulers. From 1701 to 1714 western Europe was embroiled in the War of the Spanish Succession, the last and longest of the struggles against Louis XIV of France and his policy of expansion. During these same years and after, the nations of eastern and northern Europe fought the Great Northern War (1700–1721) and watched with amazement the meteoric career of Charles XII of Sweden. Louis XIV and Charles XII both brought their countries close to ruin by their headstrong ambition, but these demonstrations of the folly that absolute monarchs could commit did not dissolve the prevailing reverence for rule by divine right.

In northeastern Europe the ambitious monarch Charles XII inherited the throne of Sweden in 1697 at sixteen years of age. Swedish imperialism had aroused resentment in neighboring lands, and Denmark, Poland, and Russia formed an alliance against the youthful king (1700). Striking back with swift and deadly strokes, Charles put Denmark out of the war in a brief campaign and turned swiftly on Russia. Before the end of the year 1700 he routed a Russian army at Narva. He then defeated the Poles, but became involved in Polish politics for five years, which gave the Russians a chance to recover. "I well know that these Swedes will beat us for a long time," Peter the Great told his troops, "but at last they will teach us how to conquer." When Charles finally decided to march on Moscow in 1708, he was too late: the chance to beat the Russians had passed. Instead of capturing Moscow the Swedes turned southward. The fierce Russian winter weakened them; and in July 1709, Peter and his improved Russian forces defeated Charles at Poltava.

Escaping to Turkey, Charles persuaded the Turks to attack the Russians; and in 1711 Peter, his army surrounded, bought peace by surrendering Azov, a Black Sea port he had captured in 1696. Charles continued his intrigues against Russia until the Turks, although they respected him, placed him under arrest. In 1714 he escaped and made his way back to Sweden. Still convinced that the Swedish forces could overcome any combination against them, he continued the exhausting struggle and took on new foes. His intractable spirit made him reject all concessions that might have secured peace, until in 1718 he was killed by a stray bullet while besieging a Norwegian fortress. Samuel Johnson wrote a fitting epitaph in *The Vanity of Human Wishes*:

> His fall was destin'd to a barren strand,
> A petty fortress, and a dubious hand;
> He left the name at which the world grew pale
> To point a moral or adorn a tale.

Peter the Great survived his obstinate opponent by seven years, but they were not happy years. This Muscovite giant (over six and one-half feet tall) found the inertia of his own subjects more frustrating than the wartime opposition of Swedes or Turks. Peter's will to concentrate power in his own hands and to reduce the army, the nobles, and the clergy to unquestioning obedience impelled him to shocking acts of cruelty. His own son, the Czarevich Alexius, was flogged to death for suspected disloyalty. "To be close to the Czar" said his subjects, "is to be close to death," and some of them came to believe that he was the Antichrist foretold in the Book of Revelation.

Yet despite occasional acts of ferocious cruelty, Peter laid the foundations of modern Russia. Though thwarted in his effort to keep an outlet on the Black Sea, he won and kept his conquests on the Baltic. By the Treaty of Nystad (1721) he secured from the exhausted Swedes a strip of coastline five hundred miles long, extending from the mouth of the Dwina to the frontier of Finland. Russia had become a Baltic power, with Baltic ports through which it could increase its trade with Europe. When Peter announced the Treaty of Nystad to his obedient senate in October 1721, he also announced that he had taken a new title. Thenceforth he chose to be known as "Father of the Fatherland, Peter the Great, Emperor of all Russia." He died four years later, and his second wife succeeded him as Catharine I.

Catharine I reigned from 1725 to 1727, then yielded the throne to Peter II, twelve-year-old grandson of Peter the Great. The boy died in 1730, and the great nobles who had used him as a pawn chose Anne, a niece of the great Peter, to succeed him. Before Anne died in 1740, she named her baby grand-nephew to follow her as Ivan VI, but within a year he was deposed and imprisoned in favor of Elizabeth II (1741–1762), daughter of Peter the Great and Catharine I. Elizabeth opposed the Germans, who had gained influence at the Russian court, and allied herself with France and Austria to fight Prussia in the Seven Years' War. As already related, Elizabeth's death in 1762 saved Frederick the Great: her successor, Peter III, admired Frederick and promptly made peace with him. This reversal filled Russia's allies with consternation and patriotic Russian hearts with disgust. The gains that Peter III threw away had cost Russia 300 thousand lives.

Peter's folly in revealing his pro-German sympathies so recklessly brought swift disaster upon him. After a reign of six months, he was dethroned and imprisoned by palace guards who helped his wife Catharine to seize control. The official version of the *coup d'état* and its outcome, as Catharine described it, did not tell the whole truth. She announced that Peter died of a colic a few days after resigning his crown.

Machiavelli, in *The Prince,*, observed realistically that a usurper who seizes a throne can never feel secure while the ruler he has deposed is still alive. There is good reason to believe that Peter III was strangled by his captors and that Catharine knew it. His death left one other deposed prince living—the unfortunate Ivan VI who had reigned briefly as a baby in 1740. When Catharine came to power in 1762 Ivan was in his early twenties and had been held in captivity since childhood. His guards had orders to kill their prisoner if an attempt were made to rescue him. Reports of such an attempt, real or feigned, reached them in 1764 and they carried out their orders.

• *Catharine's Domestic Policy* The German-born princess, who, at thirty-three, became sole autocrat of all Russia, is ranked as one of the enlightened despots. A despot she undoubtedly was: custom prescribed this role for Russian rulers. Catharine herself wrote in 1767 that "The extent of the dominion requires that the person who rules it be vested with absolute power."

Yet Catharine differed from most of her Russian predecessors in that she was well-read, sophisticated, and eager to win the approval of the western European leaders. In this respect she proved herself the most fitting successor of Peter the Great and the most enterprising executor of his policies.

In the lonely years of her early married life Catharine read eagerly the works of Voltaire, Montesquieu, and Diderot. Even as a girl she felt she must prepare herself for the great role she aspired to play in Russian affairs. She professed a deep admiration for the *philosophes* and corresponded with many of them. They in turn, happy to have a princess among their admirers, flattered Catharine excessively. "Every man of letters ought to be at your feet," Voltaire wrote her in 1765. In 1773 she invited Diderot to visit St. Petersburg, but her interviews with him did little to help her solve any material problems. "You philosophers are fortunate," she declared with justice and humor. "Your medium is paper and paper is always patient. I, Empress that I am, have to write on the sensitive skin of human beings." In practical affairs, Catharine, like Frederick the Great, remained a realist. She never permitted her doctrinaire inclinations to blind her to the fact that she had been called to rule, like an oriental despot, over an ignorant and semibarbarous people.

All the philosophers agreed that the most important reform

an enlightened sovereign could introduce was a rational code of laws. In 1767 Catharine wrote a paper entitled "Instruction to the Commission Appointed to Prepare a Draft for a New Code." Voltaire surpassed himself in his praise of it. "Lycurgus and Solon would have signed your work," he wrote, "but they would not have been capable of writing it. . . . Legislators have the first place in the temple of glory, conquerors come behind them."

Laws, as Montesquieu had observed, were "the necessary relations arising from the nature of things." Catharine hoped that it might prove possible to discover some of the natural laws on which the legislation of her empire should repose. But she and her Commission found the task more difficult than they anticipated. The discussions of the Commission dragged on interminably; it ceased to meet regularly; finally it ceased to meet at all, and the project was laid aside.

A similar fate beset most of her other domestic projects. At first she entertained a liberal plan for creating a system of provincial councils. The members were to be elected and then entrusted with the direction of their local affairs. When the councils were instituted, however, the real authority remained in the hands of a governor appointed from St. Petersburg. The reform did not bring the improvement in local administration that had been anticipated.

Catharine's professed desire to emancipate and educate the lower classes likewise failed for similar reasons. She could not overcome the inertia of nobles and bureaucrats who had little understanding of her ideas. Despite her expressions of sympathy for the Russian serfs, she permitted and contributed to an increase of serfdom during her reign. For she dared not offend the bureaucrats and the powerful privileged landholders whose support she needed to maintain her position. When she came to power she knew there had been seven changes of rule in Russia during the preceding thirty-seven years. "It is certain," the Prussian ambassador at St. Petersburg wrote Frederick the Great, "that the reign of the Empress Catharine is not to be more than a brief episode. . . ." He was mistaken: her reign was to last thirty-four years. Yet it is clear in retrospect that he had good reason to think as he did. Only an astute, courageous, and determined woman could have survived so long in a country where the government was a despotism tempered by inertia and assassination.

Inevitably there was a discrepancy between Catharine's theories and her practices. Shrewd enough to know that politics is "the art of the possible," she preferred to persuade rather than to punish. "Often it is better to inspire a reform than to enforce it," she wrote. Composing her own epitaph, she affirmed with truth that "she desired nothing but the best for her country and tried to procure for her subjects happiness, liberty, and wealth." She failed. Her reign was a golden age for the Russian nobility but it was a wretched period for the Russian serfs. As in the reign of Joseph II, this failure serves to illustrate the limitations of enlightened despotism as a mode of government. Although she possessed exceptional gifts and enjoyed autocratic powers, Catharine could not overcome the resistance of the privileged orders or free from their servitude the millions of serfs on the estates of the great landholders. The Pugachev Revolt of 1773–1775 revealed the desperation of serfs and Cossacks, but it brought no improvements in their condition—on the contrary it led Catharine to increase the repressive measures that had helped to incite a rebellion.

• *Catharine's Foreign Policy* A greater degree of success attended Catharine's diplomatic and military policies. Though born a German, she managed to acquire an intimate knowledge of the interests of her adopted country. It was her ambition to see the Russian Empire play a part in European affairs commensurate with its resources; and this ambition was strengthened by the annexation of Polish territory in 1772, which gave Russia a pretext for interfering in the Germanies. In the south, Catharine pressed a war against the Turks with such success that she had dreams of re-establishing the defunct Byzantine Empire at Constantinople. Frederick the Great, who "feared the Russians more than God," paid

Catharine a yearly subsidy; Maria Theresa invited her mediation to hasten a peaceful solution of the Potato War. Catharine's foreign policy had attained the measure of success which its consistency deserved.

Between the courts of Vienna and St. Petersburg the shadow of the Turkish question had long excited a mutual mistrust; but in 1780 Joseph decided that it was best to agree with this Muscovite adversary quickly. For the reverse which Austria had suffered in the Potato War he held French perfidy to blame, but he dared not break with his Bourbon ally while Russia remained unfriendly. Taking advantage of Catharine's notorious love of flattery, he requested permission to visit Russia in the role of Count Falkenstein, traveling without retinue or ceremony and solely for the purpose of meeting Her Imperial Majesty. Catharine "found it impossible to disguise the joy which his letter brought her," and Joseph, in the course of a visit which lasted several weeks, had the satisfaction of dispelling the spirit of unfriendliness between Austria and Russia, and of weakening Prussian influence at the Court of St. Petersburg. But the price of the understanding, inevitably, was to be Austrian assistance for Catharine's Turkish policy. Joseph's air of frankness proved no match for Catharine's feline duplicity, and the old fable of the chestnuts and the fire was to be re-enacted, with the roles reversed.

Catharine expanded the Russian frontiers while avoiding war with any of the major European powers. Her most extensive gains, made at the expense of Poland, obliterated that disordered kingdom from the map in three successive partition treaties. In the First Partition (1772) , Russia annexed 42,000, Austria 27,000 and Prussia 13,000 square miles of Polish territory. In a Second Partition (1793), without Austria, Russia added a further 96,000 and Prussia an additional 22,000 square miles. The end came in a Third Partition (1795), which gave Russia 45,000, Prussia 21,000, and Austria 18,000 square miles. In all, Catharine obtained 183,000 square miles (an area larger than the State of California) and added six million people to the population of her empire.

Two wars with Turkey (1768–1774 and 1787–1792) brought further gains although the territories proved less extensive than Catharine had hoped to win. By the Treaty of Jassy (1792) she retained the northern coast of the Black Sea and the northern slopes of the Caucasus Mountains. Russia also fought Sweden (1788–1790), though with small profit, and helped the Georgians to throw off the rule of Persia (Iran).

In her last years Catharine forgot most of her liberal ideas; the violence of the French Revolution alarmed her and she denounced it vigorously. "If the French people survive this madness," she predicted, "they will throw themselves into the arms of a strong man." She died in 1796; if she had survived four years longer she would have seen her predication vindicated by the advent of Napoleon Bonaparte.

3 Benevolent Monarchs and Reforming Ministers

• *Emperor Leopold II* As Joseph II left no children, the Hapsburg lands passed at his death to his brother Leopold, the same Leopold of Tuscany to whom he had so frequently written concerning his hopes and his anxieties. Leopold shared all Joseph's eagerness for reform but he united with it a conciliatory spirit and a talent for diplomacy. A long apprenticeship as ruler of a small principality (he became Grand Duke of Tuscany at the age of nineteen) taught him the difficulties of administrative reconstruction. In 1765, together with his young wife Marie Louise, daughter of Charles III of Spain, he took up his residence in Florence. Maria Theresa, who was always hesitant about trusting her children with authority, kept him in tutelage for five years, but after 1770 he was permitted to introduce some of the reforms which he had meditated. His enthusiasm and energy infused a new spirit into the lethargic administration of his Tuscan duchy.

Leopold's legislative program contained little that was original, nor did it need to do so. The experiments of other enlightened princes and the essays of the *philosophes* left no shortage of either precepts or examples by which he might profit. Improvements in the fiscal system enabled him to reduce taxation yet increase the revenue. Roads were built, marshes drained, new crops introduced; restrictions on trade and commerce disappeared and agriculture flourished. The wisdom of Leopold's measures rendered Tuscany one of the happiest and most prosperous of the Italian states, and earned for its ruler the flattery of the *philosophes*. Mirabeau was proud to claim him as a royal convert to physiocracy—"A convinced and unswerving disciple of the science"—and Leopold in return recognized *L'ami des hommes* as the head of the physiocratic school.

More praiseworthy even than his zeal for administrative efficiency was Leopold's activity on behalf of the most wretched class of his subjects, the criminals. Humanitarianism was a virtue much affected by the *philosophes*; they loved to pose as the champions of the oppressed, and would burst into facile tears at a tale of cruelty or injustice. Nor was their emotion altogether insincere. The brutal and stupid criminal codes of the day filled them with disgust and apprehension, and won their sympathy for the victims of the law. Eighteenth-century justice provided spectacles calculated to move the most indifferent onlooker to pity, for the cruel and unusual punishments inflicted—branding, mutilation, breaking on the wheel, hanging, drawing and quartering—were often carried out in public. The barbarity of the punishments, the arbitrary and unequal manner in which they were enforced, and the disproportion between the offences and the penalties, could hardly fail to compel the attention of thoughtful men.

Of the protests called forth by these pitiless practices the most influential was *An Essay on Crimes and Punishments* published by the Marquis Beccaria in 1764. In the name of reason and of humanity Beccaria appealed to society to alter its attitude towards the problem of crime and its repression. The purpose of the law, he urged, should not be so much the punishment of crimes as their prevention. The right of self-protection society might justly claim, the right of revenge, never. This humane reasoning was destined in time to change the whole philosophy of criminal jurisprudence. "The end of punishment," Beccaria wrote, "is no other than to prevent the criminal doing further injury to society, and to prevent others from committing the like offense." The belief that society must exact retribution on every offender against the law, even though the offense had injured nobody, he proclaimed absurd; and the spectacle of an occasional victim dragged to public execution, far from serving as a salutary warning, tended rather to brutalize and degrade the masses.

Torture as a method of forcing confessions likewise drew from Beccaria a reasoned denunciation. It was illogical, he pointed out, that the same man should be both accuser and accused, and evidence extracted under torture had been shown again and again to be unreliable. Furthermore, if the court possessed evidence sufficient to convict a man without his own confession, to extract a confession by torture was superfluous; if the court did not possess the evidence to convict the accused, then they would be torturing an innocent man. "No man can be judged a criminal until he be found guilty . . . . If he be not guilty, you torture the innocent, for in the eye of the law everyone is innocent whose crime has not been proved."

The most daring of Beccaria's recommendations, and the one which excited the loudest opposition, was his plea for the abolition of the death penalty. Public executions, with all their barbaric accompaniments of torture and mutilation, were less effective, he insisted, than lighter sentences firmly and swiftly imposed. The laws of the state should be like the laws of nature: in nature there were neither rewards nor punishments, there were only consequences; yet all rational men obeyed the laws of nature because they knew them to be universal and implacable. If criminals were convinced that a penalty, even a moderate penalty, must prove the swift and inevitable consequence of every crime, they would seldom commit an unlawful act. For as Beccaria clearly observed, "Crimes are more effectually prevented by the *certainty* than the *severity* of the punishment."

Fearing the enmity of the unenlightened, Beccaria had published his treatise anonymously, but he found support and encouragement from the Hapsburg princes who ruled in his native Italy. Leopold adopted many of his views in reforming the penal code of Tuscany; he forbade the use of torture and abolished the death penalty save in cases of parricide or *lèse-majesté*. In Austrian Lombardy, under the rule of Maximilian Franz who was Leopold's brother, the enlightened governor, Count Firmian protected Beccaria from the attacks of his enemies, and in 1768 honored him with an appointment to a chair of political philosophy at Milan.

One form of injustice, which was the most desperate and inexcusable of the age, Beccaria did not venture to attack. "The reader will perceive," he wrote toward the close of his book, "that I have omitted to discuss one class of crimes which has drenched Europe with human blood and raised up those horrible piles, where strangled cries from amid the black smoke, the crackling of human bones, and the sizzling of still palpitating bowels provide a pleasant spectacle and sweet music for the fanatical multitude. But men of understanding will appreciate that the age and the country in which I live do not permit me to inquire into the nature of this crime." Beccaria's caution was not unwarranted. The Holy Inquisition had been shorn of a great deal of its power, but it could still occasionally send a man to the stake, even in the eighteenth century. Twenty years after Beccaria wrote, Leopold had the courage, despite the opposition of the Church, to abolish the Inquisition in the duchy of Tuscany.

Praise must be accorded Leopold for the care and discretion with which he carried through his Tuscan reforms: the Marquis de Mirabeau paid tribute at the time to the "admirable prudence and infinite precautions" with which he acted. His removal to Vienna, on Joseph's death in 1790, might well have been expected to widen his sphere of activity and further the cause of enlightenment, but circumstances forced Leopold, during his short reign of two years, almost into the role of a reactionary. Joseph, on his deathbed, had withdrawn his unpopular innovations, and Leopold permitted the re-establishment of the old institutions in an effort to tranquilize the state. By a policy of mingled conciliation and firmness he was able to pacify the Hungarians, subdue the Netherlands, and conclude an honorable peace with the Turks. His sudden death in 1792 was a misfortune for the Hapsburg lands, for it occurred at a moment when the progress of the French Revolution had rendered the international situation peculiarly difficult to control, and it left the destinies of the Austrian peoples in the incapable hands of Leopold's son and heir, the Emperor Francis II. There were no further reforms; Joseph's efforts appear to have inoculated his subjects against liberal ideas, and Austria was destined to become within a quarter of a century the most reactionary of the great powers.

• *Charles III of Spain*   Like Leopold II, Charles III of Spain (1759–1788) was trained for his royal office by an apprenticeship in Italy. The untiring intrigues of his mother, Elizabeth Farnese,[1] secured for him the throne of Naples and Sicily in 1734, and for twenty-five years he strove to promote in that backward and priest-ridden state the principles of enlightened government. Charles was himself a devout Catholic; but clerical opposition to his reforms made him an enemy of the Church. With the aid of his energetic Minister Bernardo Tanucci, he labored perseveringly to reduce the power of the priesthood and to increase the prosperity of his subjects.

Called to the Spanish throne in 1759 by the death of his half-brother Ferdinand, Charles transferred his attention to the mightier task of arresting Spain's decline and turning that country from the path of decadence to which the blind policies of earlier monarchs had committed her. Stirred by stories of his benevolence the Spanish people prepared to welcome him with loyal enthusiasm, but his appearance must have disappointed them a little. Short and round-shouldered, with dark skin, small eyes, and a toothless mouth, he looked more like a broken-down clerk than a king. Court functions and military reviews interested him little. He dressed shabbily and hated ceremonies. At heart he was an administrator, a king of the

---

[1] Elizabeth Farnese, a native of Parma, was the second wife of Philip V of Spain (1700–1746). Since her son Charles appeared to have little chance of succeeding to the Spanish throne she was determined to win for him a kingdom in her native Italy.

new type, honest, conscientious, and deeply absorbed in his responsibilities. In his desire to remodel outworn institutions and to promote the welfare of his people by wise legislation he was a true prince of the Enlightenment; in his jealous retention of authority and his impatience at opposition he was a true despot.

The turbulent conditions in his capital called forth some of Charles' first efforts at reform. Madrid had all the pageantry and picturesqueness, the color and the squalor, of a medieval city. Many of the streets were narrow, dirty, and unsanitary. Badly lighted at night, without police protection, they often proved dangerous to wayfarers, for murder and robbery were common occurrences. In this favorable atmosphere private feuds flourished, for an assailant, wrapped in the anonymous security of a Spanish cloak and sombrero, could achieve his revenge and escape unrecognized, leaving the footpads to shoulder the blame for another deed of violence. In an attempt to remedy this state of affairs Charles ordered the streets cleaned and lighted, organized a police force, and forbade the wearing of long cloaks and broad-brimmed hats. But this last order, crowning as it did a series of reforms which the Spaniards regarded as foreign innovations, stirred the people of Madrid to riot and bloodshed. Frightened by the hostile demonstrations, Charles fled from the capital; the unpopular edict was withdrawn, and Leopoldo de Gregorio, Marquis of Squillaci, the minister responsible for its enforcement, was exiled in disgrace.

These Madrid riots of 1766 are of importance chiefly because they provided the anti-Jesuit party at the Court with an argument against the Society of Jesus cogent enough to discredit the latter with the king. The followers of Loyola had long been under suspicion because of their interference in political affairs. Their intrigues had led to their expulsion from Portugal in 1759 and from France in 1764. Charles, however, like the majority of his subjects, was a devout Catholic, and it was necessary to convince him that the Society of Jesus menaced his authority and his life before he could be persuaded to condemn it. The enemies of the Jesuits—members of rival orders like the Augustinians and Franciscans, *philosophes* and Masons, of whom the Count of Aranda was the leader—seized the opportunity to persuade the king that a Jesuit conspiracy was responsible for the rioting in his capital and that a plot existed to overturn his throne. There seems little reason to doubt that Charles accepted the evidence, such as it was, in good faith. In 1767 he entrusted Aranda with the task of expelling the Jesuits from Spain; the decree was carried out with a secrecy and a suddenness which left the victims no chance to resist. Among the papers seized, it is hardly necessary to add, evidence was soon "discovered" to prove that a plot to assassinate the king and all the royal family had been frustrated at the eleventh hour.

Frederick the Great, watching with shrewd eyes from the other side of Europe the fate of the Spanish Jesuits, saw more clearly than Charles the truth of the affair. He would not, he observed, go to the trouble of expelling the Jesuits from his dominions; he had need of good school teachers, and he did not suspect them of regicidal intentions. From Rome Pope Clement XIII besought the Spanish king to avoid an over-hasty judgment:

We implore Your Majesty by the sweet name of Jesus, glorious emblem of the followers of Ignatius; by the name of the Holy Virgin whose immaculate conception they have always defended; by our own advanced years we beg you to relax so great a severity, and to revoke or at least to adjourn your decree until the reasons for it can be discussed with calmness and reflection.

But Charles was unshaken. "The motives and the considerations which have driven me to take the resolution referred to, Most Holy Father," he wrote, "are too powerful and too convincing for me to consent to anything less than the expulsion from my realms of the entire order."

The Jesuits had indeed fallen upon evil days. At the election of a new pope in 1769, their enemies sought to secure from the successful candidate a promise to suppress the order entirely. Whether Clement XIV actually committed himself before election seems doubtful, but in 1773 the impatiently awaited bull was finally issued. Out of deference to the wishes of "our very dear sons, the kings of France, Spain, Portugal, and Sicily," Clement declared the Jesuits deprived of all powers, privileges, and possessions, and the order itself dissolved and extinguished forever.[1]

Despite his firmness in crushing the Jesuits, Charles wavered in his attack upon that other bulwark of the Catholic Church in Spain, the Holy Inquisition. Though he curtailed its powers and declared royal officials immune from its decrees, he could not prevent the burning of an occasional mystic or the persecution of freethinkers. The case of Don Pablo Olavide indicates how dangerous it could be to earn the displeasure of the Holy Office. The career of Olavide as a champion of the Enlightenment in eighteenth-century Spain is worth reciting here, not because he was a figure of any great importance, but because, like a cork adrift on the intellectual currents of the time, he marks the ebb and flow of the tide of rationalism and its conflict with the forces of orthodoxy.

When Charles III ascended the throne, his permission was sought by a group of intellectuals, led by the Count of Aranda, for a plan to establish agricultural colonies in the unpeopled wastes of the Sierra Morena hills. The plan called for the creation of model villages where communities would be established according to physiocratic principles, with no priests, monks, or other supposedly idle and troublesome people, but only simple, industrious citizens who would till the land happily together under a constitution based upon the laws of nature. It is at this point that Don Pablo enters the picture. As a friend of Voltaire and Rousseau, well known in some quarters and unfavorably known in others for his rationalist views, he was chosen to supervise the colonial venture. The high expectations fostered by the founders of the settlements were not realized, and in 1770 Don Pablo begged leave to re-

---

[1]The Jesuit order was reincorporated by a papal edict in 1814 but it has never regained its earlier influence.

sign his responsibilities. Unorthodox utterances and a thinly veiled contempt for the priesthood had brought him into disrepute, and in 1776 came a summons from the Inquisition. The list of charges against him included the reading of prohibited books, listening to the Mass without due respect, possessing indecent pictures and statues, and corresponding with Voltaire. The sentence of the Holy Office was eight years' imprisonment with confiscation of all property; but in 1780 Olavide was fortunate in making his escape to France, where the *philosophes* acclaimed him as a victim of priestly persecution. The epilogue to his story shows him in a different light. As a resident in France Olavide witnessed and applauded the outbreak of the Revolution, but as he watched the principles of his philosophy being translated into action he suffered a change of heart. In 1797 he returned to Spain and published his final testament, *The Gospel Triumphant, or The Conversion of a Philosopher*.

• *Pombal in Portugal* If the Portuguese kingdom enjoyed a period of enlightened despotism in the second half of the eighteenth century, the credit belongs less to Joseph I (1750–1777) than to his able but tyrannical minister, Sebastian Joseph Cavalho, Marquis of Pombal. Under the direction of this vigorous statesman the whole internal administration of Portugal was revolutionized. From 1755, the year of the great Lisbon earthquake, when Pombal's presence of mind in the face of the disaster earned him the complete confidence of his king, until the latter's death in 1777, Pombal remained the virtual dictator of Portugal. Under his direction the finances were balanced, the legal machinery simplified, and the educational system improved. In his desire to see Portugal recover something of her waning greatness, he reorganized the army and attempted to build up a stronger connection with the Portuguese colonies, a project which he sought to further by the establishment of commercial companies with special privileges. The Jesuits, already engaged in the colonial trade, resented his interference and fostered opposition to his plans both in Portugal and

America, a policy which hastened the general disaster so soon to overtake their order.

The fame which Pombal won by his energetic reforms and patriotic endeavors to liberate Portugal from foreign influences has been clouded over by the stories of his unbridled despotism. For those who ventured to oppose him he had no mercy; his political enemies spent years in secret dungeons; and he did not hesitate on occasion to strike terror into his foes by an act of summary punishment. In particular, the affair of the Tavoras, still wrapped away from the historian by terrible clouds of mystery, has invested his name with an atmosphere of horror.

On the night of September 3, 1758, as Joseph I was driving back to his palace after a love tryst, his carriage was fired upon from the shadows and the King seriously wounded. Three months later followed the arrest of the Marquis Tavora with his wife and children, the Duke of Aveiro and others, all charged with a conspiracy to assassinate the king. After a secret trial the accused were sentenced to death, the women to be beheaded, the men broken on the wheel. The sentence was carried out in public on January 3, 1759, with all the infamous ritual the law prescribed for the punishment of regicides. The secrecy surrounding the proceedings, the fact that Pombal kept in his possession the record of the trial, and the later discovery that parts of it had been destroyed led his opponents to declare the whole conspiracy an invention of his imagination. Real or imagined there is no doubt that it served him well in his war against the Jesuits. A halfcrazed Jesuit monk named Malagrida, confessor to the Tavoras, was implicated in the conspiracy and burned; and in 1759 Joseph, who was already out of patience with the Jesuits for their intrigues in his American colonies, was persuaded to banish the Order from all the dominions of the Portuguese crown.

• *Charles Frederick of Baden* The brilliant personality of Frederick the Great of Prussia has overshadowed the fame of those lesser German princes of the eighteenth century who strove to prove themselves enlightened rulers; but from such oblivion the name of Charles Frederick of Baden, at least, deserves to be retrieved. Frederick himself declared that he respected Charles above all his princely contemporaries and Frederick's judgment of men was seldom at fault.

Among the many problems to which Charles Frederick gave his attention during his long reign (1738-1811) his agrarian reforms claimed the first place. In 1769 he wrote to the Marquis de Mirabeau seeking advice on some vexatious questions of political economy. He was soon in regular communication not only with Mirabeau but with Du Pont de Nemours as well, the latter becoming for a time a member of his council and tutor to his son. This connection with the physiocrats encouraged Charles in his projects of reform and concentrated his attention on agriculture as the basis of national wealth.

Believing with Mirabeau that poor peasants make a poor kingdom and that serfdom was not only unjust but economically unsound, Charles Frederick determined to liberate all the serfs on his personal domains. He desired to establish as the foundation of the social and economic order in his state a contented class of small independent farmers. Technical improvements in agriculture, the introduction of new crops, and the encouragement of trade and manufacture enabled him to promote the prosperity of Baden while maintaining peace with his neighbors. The population was increased by settlers who came from all parts of Germany, attracted by the religious toleration and the legal protection which Charles was able to assure his subjects. At the same time an intelligent fiscal system reduced the taxation, and the progress of education and of the arts and sciences, made Baden, under Charles Frederick, one of the most prosperous and enlightened of the German states.

• *Gustavus III of Sweden* The role of Sweden in the eighteenth century was that of a second-rate power. Against a coalition of Denmark, Saxony, Russia, Prussia, Hanover, and England, not even the genius of Charles XII had been able to prevail; and the death of that defiant madman in 1718 brought the Great Northern War to a close disastrous to Sweden.[1] The loss of her Baltic provinces was a serious blow to her prestige, but more fatal still were the constitutional changes which followed the peace. In place of an absolute monarchy, the Swedes set up a government that was republican in all but name. The monarch became a puppet dignitary, while the four Estates, the nobles, clergy, burghers, and peasants, ruled by authority of a senate and a secret committee. With the rise of two political factions, the Hats, favorable to France, and the Caps, or pro-Russian party, Swedish politics became a pool of troubled waters where alien powers could fish.

A sorrier pageant of partisanship, intrigue, and venality than Stockholm presented in the mid-eighteenth century was difficult to find even in the Europe of the old regime. Governed by a fantastic constitution ("The worst conceived and most irrational that the mind of man has ever been able to devise," was Vergennes' summary of it), the Swedish state appeared to be drifting toward dissolution when a new figure came upon the scene. To Gustavus III (1771-1792) all the world was a stage. From his efforts to construct a play at the age of ten to his assassination in masquerade costume at forty-six, he was the consummate actor, and this genius for the theatrical, given scope by his exalted position, led him to dazzle the world with a display of the dramatic possibilities of kingship. He was, in Carlyle's phrase, "a *shining* sort of man," an artist in love with the kingly trade.

Gustavus was in Paris, charming the salons with his gaiety and brilliance, when the news arrived of his father's death in 1771. Delaying only long enough to conclude a secret alliance and provide for a secret pension from the French government, he started for Sweden. "He is charming and talented," conceded his uncle, Frederick the Great, to whom he paid his respects in passing, "but he will need all his patience when he

[1] See above, pp. 72-73.

reaches his native land. It is a plague of a country to govern."
The prophecy was soon justified. Gustavus appealed to the
Estates with golden oratory to forget their differences, but the
feuds remained unhealed. Convinced that only a reassertion
of the royal power could bring the discord to an end, he laid
his plans for a *coup d'état*. Isolated in his palace the night
the stroke was to fall, he organized an opera for the entertain-
ment of his enemies, and while the nobles, their suspicions
allayed, were congratulating him on his genius for stage management, the troops received their instructions. The next day
he was master of Sweden.

To the diet which met at his orders on August 21, 1772,
Gustavus spoke with a new note of authority:

> The grief which fills my heart when I contemplate the unhappy
> condition of the fatherland compels me to recall some bitter truths
> to your attention. . . . I had hoped that my persuasions would free
> you from the bonds which foreign gold, mutual hatreds, and venality,
> have drawn about you. I had hoped that the fate of other nations
> would have served as a warning to you. . . . But my pleas have left
> you unmoved, my endeavors have all been useless. I have trembled for
> the fate of my beloved country, and waited in silence the verdict of the
> nation on the conduct of its deputies. The masses of the people have
> likewise endured their burdens in silence, not knowing where to seek
> aid against so many evils, nor by what means the fatherland might be
> saved. Despair has spread throughout the kingdom until revolution
> raised its head. . . . In this crisis, when public liberty, public order,
> the very existence of the state, not to mention my own, were exposed to
> the greatest dangers, I have with the assistance of the Most High dis-
> covered a remedy for our woes. . . . I have saved my person and the
> kingdom without a single one of my subjects suffering the smallest
> hurt. . . .

The deputies listened in silence to a rebuke whose justice
they dared not deny. But as Gustavus neared the close of his
oration he appealed to his listeners with all the charm and
eloquence of which he knew himself a master, urging them to
turn their thoughts from the past to the utopia of the future:

> The one object I have in view, my dear subjects, is the re-establish-
> ment of liberty. That and only that can make you happy. When the

laws are rendered incorruptible your possessions will be safe. No longer shall any restriction be laid upon honest industry, or justice be administered in partial and arbitrary fashion. With all things working together to increase the general prosperity, a spirit of harmony will develop in town and country. Each citizen shall be left free to enjoy what is his without let or hindrance, and we shall see reborn among us a new spirit of brotherhood, a pure piety purged of all hypocrisy and all superstition.

Such was the brilliant promise that inaugurated Gustavus' new regime. Clothed with ample powers by a revised constitution, he ruled for twenty years as an enlightened despot. Under his direction the department of justice was purged and reorganized and the use of torture abolished. Religious toleration, freedom of the press, reduction of the tariff on flour and other oppressive tolls, improvements in agriculture, in education, and in the fiscal system were further triumphs of his reign. Yet not all the benefits conferred by a benevolent despot could make the nobles forget their loss of power. Their resentment deepened with the passing years until the opposition of the parliament, or *Riksdag*, of 1786 drove Gustavus to increase his dictatorial authority. Despite the open treachery of a large part of his army, he fought Russia from 1788 to 1790 and concluded an honorable peace. His matchless oratory secured him a final triumph over the *Riksdag* of 1792; but it was his last. On March 16 an anonymous letter warned him that his assassination was set for that night. A presentiment of death by violence had often troubled him and he regarded March as his most inauspicious month; but perhaps he reminded himself that the Ides of March were past, for he thrust the letter into his pocket with a faint smile and refused all precautions. At a masquerade held the same evening in the Opera House he was surrounded by a group of conspirators in black dominos who shot him in the back. He died a few days later.

Among the sovereigns of the eighteenth century Gustavus III deserves a leading place. His versatile and lively mind enabled him to organize and electrify every department of administration, and his energetic foreign policy all but regained for

Sweden that position among the Great Powers which the Northern War had cost her. His reign is known in Swedish history as the Gustavan Era; the Academy of Arts and Sciences owes its existence to his initiative, and the Swedish theatre some of its most charming dramas to his pen. To artists he was a Maecenas, or rather, since the writers of the eighteenth century delighted to pursue their classical analogies, he was the Northern Augustus. But his death provided them with an even better parallel. *C. J. Caesari virtutibus*, runs the inscription to his collected writings, *et fato similis*: like unto C. J. Caesar in his virtues and in his fate.

• *Struensee in Denmark-Norway* Not even the decrepit Dano-Norwegian state,[1] lying on the outskirts of Europe and consecrated to decay, was destined to escape the rough hand of the eighteenth-century reformer. It is true that the Danish annals of the period make little boast of enlightened monarchs. For generations a Christian had succeeded a Frederick and a Frederick a Christian in monotonous succession, while abuses multiplied until there was little if anything that was not rotten in the state of Denmark. Nevertheless, the early years of the reign of Christian VII (1766–1808) were marked by some daring reforms, the work not of the king (he had debauched himself to the point of imbecility) but of a royal favorite, Johann Friedrich von Struensee.

From the dignity of court physician, Struensee rose in favor until he became chief councilor of the incapable king and the queen's acknowledged lover. A kingdom had become his plaything and ambition urged him to essay the role of enlightened despot. To clear his way he swept aside the antiquated Council of State and reorganized the departments of government, removing from power any officials who ventured to oppose his projects. Between March 1771, and January 1772, over a thousand cabinet orders flowed from his pen, orders which left few Danish institutions undisturbed. Many of the

---

[1]The crowns of Denmark and Norway were united from 1397 until 1814.

reforms were sound in principle and highly beneficial in their effects, as a short summary of the most important must indicate; but Struensee's drastic methods of procedure and his disregard of criticism angered an increasing number of the Danish people.

To the ranks of his enemies were soon added a host of ex-officials, driven from their sinecures by the rigid economy of his fiscal policy. Undeterred by their protests, Struensee held his course until he had reduced the finances to order and balanced the budget. With the same thoroughness he over-hauled the judicial system, abolished torture, and revised and ameliorated the penal code. All classes were promised the benefits of equality before the law, religious toleration, pro-motion on a basis of merit, free labor, and free trade. To meet the problems of sanitation and public health, which held for him with his physician's training a particular interest, Struen-see instituted a system of hospitals and clinics, and a program of public hygiene unique in eighteenth-century Europe.

The presumption of this minister, who acted with the insolence of a royal despot but lacked the divinity that doth hedge a king, invited a counterstroke on the part of his foes. It came in January 1772. Christian VII, liberated from a tutelage that had become virtually an imprisonment, was persuaded to sign an order for the arrest of his chief minister, and Struensee was seized in his sleep. Two months later he paid for his usurpation of power on the block; but although the reactionaries annulled his decrees they could not altogether undo his work. His reforms had broken through the entrench-ments of the old regime in Denmark and opened the way for new influences and new ideas. It was a virtue of many ideals of the Enlightenment that they persisted on their own merits even when their advocates perished.

• *Turgot in France*   It is a fact not without irony that while French philosophers were instructing all the princes of Europe in statecraft, their own government remained a stronghold of privilege, incompetence, and corruption. Throughout the

eighteenth century the prestige of the French monarchy continued to decline at home and abroad. Louis XV (1715–1774)
forsook the business of state for his mistresses and his mas-
querades; to the warnings of his ministers that the monarchy
was drifting to destruction he is credited with the reply that
the machine would last out his day and after him the deluge.
So the French peasantry continued to groan beneath the
burdens of an obsolete manorial system while at Paris a gay
and extravagant court dazzled the eyes of Europe with the
brilliance of decay.

The accession of Louis XVI (1774–1792) was hailed throughout France as an omen of better days. "Any novelty,"
Frederick the Great observed cynically, "is popular with the
French." But when the new monarch appointed as his Comptroller General the honest and courageous Turgot even the
Prussian king was impressed. "I have heard high praise of M.
Turgot," he wrote D'Alembert. "They say he is a man, wise,
honest, and industrious. So much the better for your poor
peasants. If he has a heart in his breast he will lighten the
burden of their taxes." For twenty months Turgot fought to
reform the administration until a combination of the Church,
the *Parlement*, and the nobles overthrew him. His fall sealed
the fate of the French monarchy. All possibility of a peaceful
revolution having failed, it became merely a matter of time
until a popular insurrection would break the yoke of privilege.

The nemesis of the monarchy, and the final cause of its
destruction, was insolvency. Turgot's proclamation on taking
charge of the finances: "No bankruptcy, no increase of taxation,
no loans," was a bold attempt to face this problem squarely.
One expedient and one alone could render his program prac-
ticable, and that was a drastic reduction of expenditures. Any
attempt at retrenchment, however, was certain to stir up such a
cloud of parasites as would darken the sun. "There is no abuse
that does not give someone a livelihood," Turgot wrote; and
he knew that his only defense against his enemies would be
the dubious buckler of the king's favor. He has been accused
of forcing through his reforms with too great impetuosity; but

none knew so well as he how precarious his tenure of office might prove. Like most of his fellow *philosophes* he saw nothing wrong in using despotic power in the cause of liberty. "Give me five years of despotism," is the prayer attributed to him, "and France shall be free." He was to have twenty months.

To the list of malcontents caused by the abridgment of sinecures and curtailment of pensions were soon added more powerful foes. The queen, Marie Antoinette, resented the limitations Turgot sought to impose on her expenditures; the Church feared his efforts on behalf of religious toleration; and the *Parlement* of Paris, recalled despite Turgot's protest in 1774, reasserted its ancient right of obstructing legislation. Fortune herself appeared unfavorable, for the decree establishing the freedom of the wheat trade, which Turgot, true to his physiocratic principles, had made one of his first concerns, was followed by rioting and famine. To the measures which he urged upon the king for the suppression of the rioters Louis gave firm assent; but the outbreak of disturbances caused apparently by the radical legislation of the new minister damaged the latter's prestige. Admirers, who a few months earlier had hailed Turgot as a Solon about to introduce a new age of gold, began to question the wisdom of his measures; and the king himself, not for the first time, was visited by doubts.

On January 5, 1776, Turgot laid before the Royal Council six edicts embodying the reforms which he considered most imperative. Four of the decrees involved fiscal proposals of a secondary importance; but two—the abolition of the *corvée* and the suppression of the trade guilds—were revolutionary in their implications. The *corvée* was a method of forced labor whereby the peasants were compelled to spend twelve to fifteen days a year repairing the roads, a service from which the nobility and gentry derived the chief advantage. Turgot planned to convert this compulsory labor into a tax or money payment, and had he proposed to levy the assessment only on those classes of citizens subject to the *corvée* he might have carried his point. His aim, however, as he frankly stated, was to assess the nobility and clergy, hitherto exempt from such taxes, on an equal basis with the peasants. To a decree which challenged their immunity in so audacious a fashion the privileged classes closed their ranks in implacable opposition.

The edict for the suppression of the trade guilds drew upon Turgot denunciations no less bitter from members of the bourgeoisie. These guilds, which dated for the most part from the Middle Ages, were exclusive industrial corporations unsuited to the economic conditions of the eighteenth century. The masters of a guild, possessing a monopoly in the manufacture and sale of various necessary commodities, could enrich themselves at the expense of the public welfare. Furthermore, their statutes authorized them to limit the number of workers engaged in a trade and to prevent an artisan, however skilled, from practicing his profession unless he were a guild member. All these restrictions and privileges Turgot attempted to sweep away in a single edict. The guilds, he insisted, must be dissolved; workmen were to be left free to practice whatever trade they wished; and any union of masters, journeymen, or apprentices was to be held illegal.

When the *Parlement* refused to register the Six Edicts, Turgot appealed to the king. Accordingly, at a *lit de justice* held March 12, 1776, Louis went through the ceremony of appearing before the *Parlement* in person and commanding the chamber to register the decrees. The *Parlement*, according to accepted precedent, had no course but to comply; refusal would have had no effect save perhaps to draw upon the members a sentence of exile to their country estates. At the end of five hours the last decree had been read and accepted, but Turgot's triumph was a hollow one. His influence, already undermined, had been strained too far by this display of authority; his only shield was the king's favor and Louis chose this moment to abandon him. Refusing to recognize that his ministry was over, Turgot wrote the king again and again begging him to awe the rebellious *Parlement* into a proper submission and dare to carry out the necessary reforms. "Do not forget, Sire," he counseled, "it was weakness that brought the head of Charles I to the block. . . ." But Louis avoided a meeting with his Comptroller General, and when he finally wrote him on May 12 it was to request his resignation. Forced into retirement Turgot had to watch in silence the exultation of his enemies and the annulment of his decrees. He died in 1781; had he survived a few years longer he might have witnessed the bloody triumph of Liberty, Equality, and Fraternity, and mourned the death of the irresolute king his prescience could not save.

● *From Reform to Revolution* Through a study of the enlightened despots and their reforms it becomes evident that European institutions in the eighteenth century were everywhere in need of renovation. The general similarity of the various reform programs and the fact that they were supported by a consistent philosophy prove that enlightened men in each country recognized the prevalent evils and were in substantial agreement as to the best remedies to apply to them. The one point about which some uncertainty persisted was the question to whom the task of remodeling society might most happily be entrusted.

When political innovations are undertaken by an existing government on its own behalf they are known as reforms; when they are introduced in defiance of the government and lead to its overthrow they constitute a revolution. In general the political thinkers of the eighteenth century favored the method of reform. They endorsed monarchy as the most satisfactory type of government and they regarded a despot as peculiarly fitted to carry through the reform program. The monarchs for the most part were ready to undertake this duty. Could they have secured the wholehearted support of their subjects they might have reconstructed the old regime and adapted its institutions to meet newer requirements. To a certain extent this is what did happen in Sweden, in Spain, in Austria, and in Prussia.

Yet the far-reaching alterations which the time demanded, even when carried out by royal authority, were nonetheless revolutionary in their scope. The enlightened despots by their reforming zeal set a dangerous example to their subjects. Their legislative experiments when successful taught the people to desire better government; when they failed they left a deepened consciousness of existing evils. More effectively even than the *philosophes*, these reforming monarchs taught contempt for privilege and tradition. Their ruthless suppression or modification of established institutions—of the Inquisition, the feudal courts, the trade guilds—dispelled the veneration with which men had regarded these august survivals of medievalism. It is difficult to tear down part of a building without endangering the rest. When so many ancient institutions were being weighed in the balance and found wanting, monarchy also was certain sooner or later to be faced with the ordeal of justifying itself before the bar of rationalism. This menace was implicit in the reform philosophy from the first but it is only when it proclaimed itself in a manner rude and unmistakable that the reform movement can be dignified with the name of revolution. The refusal of the French States-General in 1789 to disband "until they had given France a constitution" was a direct challenge to a despotic monarchy and thus marks the opening of the revolutionary era.

As reflected in philosophical speculation (the philosophy of the eighteenth century was a pool in which coming events cast their shadows) the transition from reform proposals to revolutionary doctrines may be discerned with the publication of Rousseau's *Social Contract* in 1762. By his insistence that sovereignty resides not with the monarch but with the people Rousseau suggested a counterauthority by which reforms might be invoked and executed; a substitute horse as it were that might be yoked to the reform chariot. The theories of the Social Contract and Popular Sovereignty reduced a king and his ministers to the status of magistrates responsible to the people, and liable, if they failed in their duties, to be relieved of their delegated authority. In summing up the obligations of a ruler to his subjects, Rousseau wrote:

What we have said makes it clear . . . that the depositaries of the executive power are not the people's masters, but its officers; that it can set them up and pull them down when it likes; that for them there is no question of contract, but of obedience; and that in taking charge of the functions the state imposes on them they are doing no more than fulfilling their duty as citizens, without having the remotest right to argue about the conditions.

In the eighteenth century, France, alone of the larger European nations, failed to experience the benefits of enlightened despotism. Disabused of the temptation to put their trust in princes, the French people were the first to cast about for a different solution to their difficulties. The reforms—establishment of civil equality and religious toleration, destruction of privileges, of trade restrictions, of feudal dues, of serfdom—which in other countries were attempted singlehanded by the sovereign princes, in France, when all other efforts had failed, were to be carried through by the authority of the sovereign people.

Epilogue: The Enlightened Despotism of Napoleon

In 1764 Voltaire made an interesting prediction in a letter to a friend. He wrote:

Everything I observe is sowing the seeds of a revolution that will inevitably come to pass and which I shall not have the pleasure of witnessing. The French always get there late but at last they do arrive. By degrees enlightenment has spread so widely that it will burst forth at the first opportunity, and then there will be a grand commotion: The younger generation are lucky: they will see some great things.

Twenty-five years passed before the predicted revolution engulfed France in 1789. Its mounting fury swept away much of the old regime and overturned the French throne, but it failed to produce an orderly republican government to replace the discarded monarchy. From 1789 to 1799 the lawyers, orators, legislators, and constitution makers tried—and failed—to create and preserve a stable administration. Then the French people turned from the discredited politicians to the successful military leaders. In 1799 a *coup d'état* placed Napoleon Bonaparte, most brilliant commander of the French revolutionary armies, at the head of the state.

Napoleon combined in himself the spirit of the Enlightenment and the energy of the Revolution—he had, as he said, "swallowed all the formulas." He is not usually included with the enlightened despots of the eighteenth century—he was not, after all, a hereditary or legitimate monarch. But he admired Frederick the Great, and his achievements as an organizer and administrator fulfilled many of the projects the eighteenth-century philosophers had urged.

To his task of restoring France to order Napoleon brought a brain and character superbly fitted for command. His tireless mind grasped the essentials of a problem with astonishing ease—his thoughts, he said with justice, moved in perpendiculars where most people think in diagonals. On the battlefield he could make immediate and inspired decisions, but he was equally impressive in patient, intellectual deliberations. He could ask, "Do you know what I most admire in this world? It is the total inability of force to organize anything." And he could affirm with conviction that "The true conquests, the only ones that leave no regrets, are those that are won from ignorance."

To the French, and to many Europeans, Bonaparte in his first years appeared almost a demigod. The German poet Goethe wrote:

> What centuries have dimly meditated
> His mind perceives in brightest clarity.

Metternich, certainly not a friendly critic, admitted that "whilst in his conceptions all was clear and precise, in what required action he knew neither difficulty nor uncertainty."

Although he adopted many of the reforms the *philosophes* had proposed, Napoleon showed scant respect for most of the theorists and reformers of the Enlightenment. "He had the greatest contempt for the false philosophy and false philanthropy of the eighteenth century," Metternich recalled. "Among the chief teachers of these doctrines, Voltaire was the special object of his aversion." Rousseau fascinated Napoleon in his youth, but later Napoleon repudiated him with the remark, "Your Rousseau was a madman." His often-quoted epigram when he came to power, "The romance of the Revolution is over; we must begin in history," emphasized his contempt for those he described as "phrasemakers" and "idealogues."

Yet it is clear in historical retrospect that, despite his extraordinary energy and ability, Napoleon could not have gained eminence if the way had not been prepared. The writings of the *philosophes*, calling for an inspired legislator, an enlightened despot, to establish a rational state of society, helped to set the stage for Napoleon's arrival. Albert Vandal observed perceptively, *L'idée a précédé l'homme* (the idea preceded the man).

An executor of the Revolution, Napoleon consolidated the legislation adopted piecemeal during the ten years of turmoil from 1789 to 1799. The reforms of the Revolution were in the main the reforms which had been demanded earlier by the *philosophes*[1] and Napoleon knew what France desired. The establishment of civil equality received its sanction in the famous *Code Napoléon*. The multitude of law courts and clerical courts with their overlapping jurisdiction gave place to a single uniform system of legal administration. Religious toleration was confirmed, although the First Consul concluded a Concordat with Pope Pius VII which restored France to the Catholic Church. The internal tariffs that had constricted trade and the oppressive and unequal taxes that had exempted the privileged and burdened the unprivileged had been abolished early in the Revolution and were not restored.

French national finances, ruinously mismanaged before 1789, dissolved into chaos during the Revolution. Successive decrees authorized the printing of paper money until inflation rendered the notes worthless. One of Napoleon's first reforms concerned the restoration of a sound currency. He insisted that his government must remain solvent and he founded the Bank of France to assist in regulating the economy.

The revolutionary legislators had given much thought to education but lack of funds and of teachers handicapped their plans. Here too Napoleon gave an incomplete project the stamp of his authoritarian mind. Primary, secondary, and higher education were to be coordinated and secularized. At the same time, however, he relaxed the laws against the religious orders, and scores of religious schools, closed during the Revolution, reopened under his rule.

The desire of the French people in 1789 has been described

---

[1] See above, pp. 27–32.

as "an intense aspiration for order." Under Napoleon's firm administration they had order. They found their liberties reduced but their security increased. As First Consul Napoleon approximated the *philosophes'* concept of an enlightened ruler, although his rule proved more harsh and rigid than liberal thinkers desired. Yet there can be little doubt that a majority of the French people preferred Napoleon's enlightened dictatorship to the violence and anarchy of the Revolution. In 1802 a popular plebiscite made him Consul for life and in 1804 a further plebiscite made him Emperor of the French.

"One thing he always regretted extremely," Metternich remembered about Napoleon, "was that he could not take the principle of legitimacy as the basis of his power. Few men have been so profoundly conscious as he was that authority deprived of this foundation is precarious and fragile, and open to attack." Napoleon himself, looking back on his career from St. Helena, described the situation in more dramatic terms. "Throughout my whole reign," he admitted, "I was the keystone of an edifice entirely new and resting on the most slender foundations. Its duration depended on the issue of my battles. I was never, in truth, master of my movements; I was never at my own disposal."

Although he mocked at visionaries, Napoleon was a romancer himself. "I often used to amuse myself at daydreaming," he admitted more than once, "in order afterwards to measure my dreams with the calipers of reason." The dream he conceived of establishing a Bonaparte dynasty that would hold half of Europe under French domination suggests the limitations of his genius. As his power increased his thoughts became more traditional and stereotyped. To replace the legitimate Bourbon dynasty of France by an upstart Corsican clan, to marry a Hapsburg archduchess after defeating her father's armies four times, to imagine that such a hybrid regime could endure and that Europe would accept it—this was to daydream too defiantly, and fail to measure the dream with the calipers of reason.

How did Napoleon view himself and his career after his downfall, when he had leisure to contemplate it in retrospect?

He labored to fashion the legend that as the Son of the Revolution he had carried out the mandate of the Enlightenment. He did not deny that his rule had been authoritarian, his government a dictatorship. But he argued that no other method of rule was available to him. "The world begged me to govern it," he insisted, and he felt confident that the judgment of history would vindicate his decisions.

Posterity will do me justice. The truth will be known; and the good I have done will be compared with the faults I have committed. Had I succeeded, I would have died with the reputation of the greatest man that ever existed. As it is, although I have failed, I shall be considered an extraordinary man: my elevation was unparalleled.

It is easy to see in retrospect that Napoleon rose to power because the French Revolution became militarized. Having tried, and failed, to bring to birth the utopia of their dreams, the generation of 1789 turned for compensation to war and conquest, to the empire and the glory. Like Napoleon himself, the young men who in 1789 had gone forth to seek virtue turned back to marry power. The Napoleonic legend was not the creation of one man; it was the achievement of several generations. The idealized concept of the philosopher-prince prefigured it. The Romantic Movement, which transformed art and literature, found its political and military expression in the revolutionary debates and the Napoleonic battles. "What a romance my life has been," Napoleon mused when it was ending, recognizing that it was a union of poetry and politics which had shaped his opportunity and his legend. He compared himself to the lonely Titan whose fate captured the imagination of all the Romantic poets. "A new Prometheus," he exclaimed, "I am nailed to a rock to be gnawed by a vulture. Yes, I have stolen the fire of heaven and made a gift of it to France. The fire has returned to its source and I am here."

The high-flown language, the classical analogies, ring strangely on twentieth-century ears. But they were a product, as Napoleon himself was a product, of eighteenth-century concepts and ideals. He too had been touched in fugitive moments by the nostalgic dream of an idyllic society, of semirural communities where people would find happiness under just laws and satisfy their simple needs in a pastoral paradise. But his realism told him that the poets' Arcadia was a fusion of childhood memory and romantic aspiration. As a literary device the tradition of life as a bucolic idyll had been known since classical times. But the revival of this tradition in the eighteenth century, the plea for a return to nature, was tinged with historical fatality, for the dream was about to fade beyond recapture. The industrial revolution, and the "dark satanic mills," lay in wait for the subsequent generations.

Unlike most of his contemporaries, the fallen emperor possessed the prescience to realize that within his lifetime something immemorially consoling to the human heart had begun to disappear. European man's ancient partnership with the earth, that close communion which had shaped a thousand generations, was nearing its close. Life, for the millions still unborn, would be increasingly a life in the city, the stars shut out, the rhythm of the seasons supplanted by the rhythm of machines. "A person who has lost the room in which he was born," Napoleon observed, "the garden where he played as a child, the house of his forebears—such a person has no fatherland." To his brooding mind it appeared that the old agrarian awareness of a "rooted security" had already begun to dissolve. "This kind of happiness can scarcely be known in today's France except as tradition has passed it on," he insisted. "The Revolution has overturned everything; it has deprived the older generation of that happiness, and the new generation has never known it."

Utopia, being the stuff that dreams and memories are made of, survived the fury and disillusionment of the Revolution, and emerged again from the turbulent years shining and indestructible as ever. But now it lay in the past. As the young men who had seen visions became old men dreaming dreams, Europe of the old regime, softened by distance, took on the colors of the lost Arcadia. "Only those who were alive before 1789," conceded the aging Talleyrand, "know how pleasant life can be."

Bibliographical Note

This note will discuss two trends that are influencing current appraisals of the Enlightenment, and will then cite about one hundred books that should be helpful to the student who wishes to read more widely. It is not possible to do more than suggest, in these few pages, the extensive research and the thousands of books that have been devoted to the history of the eighteenth century.

One significant trend in recent history writing has been the recognition that a civilization may prove a more "intelligible field of historical study" than a single political state. This argument is not new, but it was given new emphasis by Arnold J. Toynbee in his monumental work, *A Study of History*, the ten volumes of which were published between 1934 and 1954. One consequence of the effort to identify and delineate entire civilizations has been the tendency to link the development of Europe and America under captions such as the "Western" or the "Atlantic" civilization. Readers who desire to know more of current trends in history writing will find them discussed in *History*, by John Higham, Leonard Krieger, and Felix Gilbert (Englewood Cliffs, N. J., 1965), and in *History in a Changing World* (Norman, Okla., 1956), by Geoffrey Barraclough.

The quest for a more meaningful synthesis is reflected in *The new Cambridge Modern History*. The original series appeared over half-a-century ago, and allotted four of its thirteen volumes to the hundred years 1715-1815, entitling them *The Eighteenth Century, The United States, The French Revolution,* and *Napoleon*. In *The New Cambridge Modern History* such milestones as 1789, 1799, and 1815 have less significance. Three out of twelve volumes cover 117 years (1713–1830), and are named *The Old Regime, 1713–1763, The American and French Revolutions, 1763–1793*, and *War and Peace in an Age of Upheaval, 1793–1830*.

The American counterpart to the *Cambridge Modern History* is "The Rise of Modern Europe" series, edited by William L. Langer. The reader will find this series a valuable aid. The three volumes that cover the period 1715-1789 are available in hard cover and paperbound (Torchbook) editions. They are: *The Quest for Security, 1715–1740* by Penfield Roberts (New York, 1947), *Competition for Empire, 1740–1763* by Walter L. Dorn (New York, 1940), and *From Despo'ism to Revolution, 1763–1789* by Leo Gershoy (New York, 1944). Although the series as a whole retains the older Europocentric focus, this does not reduce its usefulness for the careers and characters of the enlightened despots. Critical bibliographical essays conclude each volume, most of which have been updated since their initial publication.

A bold and scholarly effort to link intellectual and political movements in Europe and America as manifestations of a common striving and stimulus has been made by Robert R. Palmer. His two-volume analysis and exposition, *The Age of the Democratic Revolution: A Political History of Europe and America, 1760-1800* (Princeton, N.J. 1959-64) identifies the common aspirations that shaped developments while acknowledging the variant expressions these aspirations took. Across the Atlantic, Jacques L. Godechot, inspired by similar views, has questioned whether the French Revolution should not be regarded as one phase of a vaster occidental revolution that leavened all Western civilization in the later decades of the eighteenth century. His argument is often linked with Palmer's as the Palmer-Godechot thesis or interpretation.

Within this expanded frame or pattern, the enlightened despotism of the eighteenth century ceases to be a unique or independent movement. It becomes one of many strands in an intricate and far flung web. One might seek, for instance, in the Americas for evidence that enlightened despotism found some advocates and some influence there. The term "enlightened despots," however, still retains its limited and traditional connotation. As characters of the eighteenth-century drama, the enlightened despots may be defined as a group of legitimate European princes, who endorsed "enlightened" policies, and sought to appease the criticism and social discontent of their time by judicious reforms imposed from above.

A second trend in historical interpretation, which should be noted here, is the disposition to regard the *philosophes*, and the princes whom they advised, as more realistic and practical than many earlier writers believed them to be. This change of view may be gauged by comparing Carl Becker's provocative and persuasive essay, *The Heavenly City of the Eighteenth Century Philosophers*, with such recent scholarly studies as *Voltaire's Politics: the Poet as Realist* by Peter Gay (Princeton, N. J., 1959), or with *Enlightened Bureaucracy Versus Enlightened Despotism in Baden, 1750–1792* by Helen P. Liebel (Philadelphia, 1965).

For further authoritative books on the leading actors, and on special aspects of the eighteenth-century enlightenment, the reader will find *A Guide to Historical Literature* useful (New York, 1961). Unfortunately the organization is cumbrous and the index confusing. A more specific guide for works, especially recent works, on the later eighteenth century, is *Les Révolutions, 1770–1799* by Jacques L. Godechot (Paris, 1963), translated by Herbert H. Rowen as *France and the Atlantic Revolution of the Eighteenth Century, 1770–1799* (New York, 1965).

THE EIGHTEENTH CENTURY

Old treatments, but still very much worth reading, are H. A. Taine, *The Ancient Regime* (New York, 1896), Alexis de Tocqueville, *The Old Regime and the Revolution*, in a new translation by Stuart Gilbert (New York, 1955), and Albert Sorel's summary of the century in the first volume of his monumental *L'Europe et la Révolution Française*, 9 vols. (Paris, 1895–1911). His eighteenth-century summary is now available in English as a paperback (Torchbook). Other good one-volume treatments are David Ogg, *Europe of the Ancient Regime, 1715-1783*, (Meridian, Cleveland, 1965), Matthew S. Anderson, *Europe in the Eighteenth Century, 1713-1783* (New York, 1962), and R. J. White, *Europe in the Eighteenth Century* (New York, 1965). Somewhat more specialized studies of classes and conditions are Henri Sée, *Economic and Social Conditions in France During the Eighteenth Century* (New York, 1927); Albert Goodwin, *The European Nobility in the Eighteenth Century* (London, 1953); Franklin L. Ford, *Robe and Sword: The Regrouping of the French Aristocracy After Louis XIV* (Cambridge, Mass., 1953); and Elinor G. Barber, *The Bourgeoisie in 18th Century France* (Princeton, N. J., 1955).

THE INTELLECTUAL CLIMATE OF OPINION

Harald Höffding, *A History of Modern Philosophy*, 2 vols. (New York, 1950); Books 4 and 5 of Vol. 1 are relevant for the Enlightenment. The best one-volume summary of political ideas in English is George H. Sabine, *History of Political Theory*, (New York, 1961), especially chapters 27 and 28. For more specific treatises, consult Ernst Cassirer, *The Philosophy of the Enlightenment*, (Boston, 1955), and Paul Hazard, *European Thought in the Eighteenth Century From Montesquieu to Lessing* (New Haven, Conn., 1954). Among older studies still valuable are: Kingsley Martin, *French Liberal Thought in the Eighteenth Century* (London, 1929; 2d edition London, 1954) and available as a paperback (Torchbook); F. de la Fontainerie, *French Liberalism and Education in the Eighteenth Century* (New York, 1933); Preserved Smith, *History of Modern Culture*, Vol. 2 (New York, 1934), now also a Torchbook paperback; Carl Becker, *The Heavenly City of the Eighteenth-Century Philosophers* (New Haven, Conn., 1932) which has run to a dozen editions; Basil Willey, *The Eighteenth Century Background* (London, 1940), which is now paperback with the subtitle *Studies on the Idea of Nature in the Thought of the Period.*

For comparison of older with more recent analyses, see Harold Nicolson, *The Age of Reason: the Eighteenth Century* (Garden City, N. Y., 1965) and W. H. Coates, H. V. White, and J. S. Schapiro, *An Intellectual History of Western Europe* (New York, 1966), giving special attention to Vol. I, Book 2, "Formation of the Modern Mind in the Eighteenth Century." The temper of the time is also thoughtfully dissected in George R. Havens, *The Age of Ideas: from Reaction to Revolution in Eighteenth Century France* (New York, 1955); Peter Gay, *The Party of Humanity: Essays on the French Enlightenment* (New York, 1963); and Gerald R. Cragg, *Reason and Authority in the Eighteenth Century* (New York, 1964). Cragg also discusses religion in *The Church and the Age of Reason* (New York, 1961). One may add Robert R. Palmer's thoughtful study, *Catholics and Unbelievers in Eighteenth Century France* (Princeton, N. J., 1939) and Henri Daniel-Rops, *The Church in the Eighteenth Century*, translated by John Warrington (New York, 1964). How faith in the future of man developed has been related by John B. Bury, *The Idea of Progress* (reprinted, 1960), while the doubts that underlie the general optimism of the age are analyzed by Henry Vyverberg in *Historical Pessimism in the French Enlightenment* (Cambridge, Mass. 1958).

MONARCHY AND STATECRAFT

For a study of monarchy, the following books are helpful: Henri Frankfurt, *Kingship and the Gods: a study of Ancient Near Eastern Religion as the Integration of Nature and Society* (Chicago, 1948); Harold Nicolson, *Kings, Courts and Monarchy* (New York, 1962); John Neville Figgis, *The Divine Right of Kings* (Torchbook). In addition Franz Neumann's, *The Democratic and Authoritarian State* (Glencoe, Ill., 1957) has illuminating essays on absolutism. Friedrich Meinecke's, *History of Machiavellianism* (London, 1957) traces the concept of "reasons of state." For the French court of the eighteenth century there is a book by George P. Gooch, *Louis XV: the Monarchy in Decline* (New York, 1956). The influence exercised by Louis's mistress, Madame de Pompadour, is described in two recent biographies by David Mynders Smythe and by Nancy Mitford, both published in New York in 1953.

PHILOSOPHERS, CRITICS, AND REFORMERS

For criticism of the French monarchy before 1715, consult Lionel Rothkrug, *Opposition to Louis XIV: The Political and Social Origins of the French Enlightenment* (Princeton, N. J., 1965). Further useful studies are Howard Robinson, *Bayle the Sceptic* (New York, 1931); John W. Gough, *John Locke's Political Philosophy* (New York, 1950); Ernest C. Mossner, *The Life of David Hume* (Austin, Texas, 1954); and Albert Sorel, *Montesquieu* (Chicago, 1888). On Voltaire, consult Peter Gay, *Voltaire's Politics: the Poet as Realist* (Princeton, N. J., 1959), cited above and Norman L. Torrey, *The Spirit of Voltaire* (New York, 1938). The most exhaustive study is by Gustave Le B. Desnoiresterres, *Voltaire et la société au XVIIIe siècle*, 2d edition, 8 vols. (Paris, 1871–1896). For Diderot, see Lester G. Crocker, *The Embattled Philosopher, a Biography of Denis Diderot* (East Lansing,

Mich., 1954), and Arthur M. Wilson, *Diderot: the Testing Years, 1713–1759* (New York, 1957), both of which may be supplemented by the much older but still helpful work of John Morley, *Diderot and the Encyclopaedists*, 2 vols. (New York, 1878). D'Alembert has attracted much less interest, but there is a good French biography by Joseph L. F. Bertrand, *D'Alembert* (Paris, 1899). William H. Wickwar has done justice to a lesser figure in *Baron d'Holbach: a Prelude to the French Revolution* (London, 1935); John M. S. Allison has written about *Lamoignon de Malsherbes* (New Haven, Conn., 1938); and Pierre Jolly described *Du Pont de Nemours, soldat de la liberté* (Paris, 1956). For the physiocrats there is the old, brief, but still interesting account by Henry Higgs, *The Physiocrats* (London, 1897), and the more recent works by Georges Weulersse, *Les physio-crates* (Paris, 1931) and *Le mouvement physiocratique en France de 1756 à 1770*, 2 vols. (Paris, 1910). Both these studies are in French, but Douglas Dakin has prepared an English biography of Turgot, *Turgot and the Ancien Régime in France* (London, 1939). Rousseau has been left to the last here because today, as in his own time, he tends to stand alone. Frederick C. Green, *Jean-Jacques Rousseau: a Critical Study of His Life and Writings* (New York, 1955), and Ernst Cassirer, *The Question of Jean-Jacques Rousseau* (New York, 1954) may be consulted, together with the older work by Alfred Cobban, *Rousseau and the Modern State* (London, 1934). For the theory, exalted by Rousseau, that man was more virtuous in a state of nature, see H. N. Fairchild, *The Noble Savage* (New York, 1928).

FREDERICK THE GREAT

There is a biography of Frederick's intimidating father by Robert R. Ergang, *The Potsdam Führer, Frederick William I* (New York, 1941), and an account of the latter's methods of government by Reinhold A. Dorwart, *The Administrative Reforms of Frederick William I of Prussia* (Cambridge, Mass., 1953). George P. Gooch has provided a sane and well-compressed life of the son in *Frederick the Great: the Ruler, the Writer, the Man* (New York, 1947); and a French biography by Pierre Gaxotte has been translated by R. A. Bell as *Frederick the Great* (London, 1941). The best and most de-tailed earlier life is that of Reinhold Koser, *Geschichte Friedrichs des*

Grossen, 4th and 5th editions, 4 vols. (Berlin, 1912–1914). For a general description of German life in Frederick's time, consult Walter H. Bruford, *Germany in the Eighteenth Century: the Social Background of the Literary Revival* (Cambridge, England, 1935); for the question of Frederick's influence in strengthening authoritarianism in German life see Leonard Krieger, *The German Idea of Freedom* (Boston, 1957).

CATHERINE THE GREAT

For Catherine's most energetic predecessor, Peter I, Benedict H. Sumner's *Peter the Great and the Emergence of Russia* (New York, 1951) is sound and well condensed. George P. Gooch treats Catherine fairly in *Catherine the Great and Other Studies* (New York, 1954). The relations between Russia and western Europe are reflected in *Russia in the Intellectual Life of Eighteenth Century France* by Dmitri S. von Mohrenschildt (New York, 1936). For the conspiracy that made Catherine empress, and conditions at her court, *The Memoirs of Princess Dashkov* (London, 1958) are spirited and revealing. Catherine's own memoirs are listed below under Contemporary Sources. Stanislas Augustus Poniatowski, whom Catherine made king of Poland, is described against the background of the Enlightenment by Jean Fabre, *Stanislas-Auguste Poniatowski et l'Europe des lumières: étude de cosmopolitanisme* (Paris, 1952).

JOSEPH II

For the long reign of Joseph's mother, Maria Theresa, the best source material in print is the collection of documents assembled by Alfred, Ritter von Arneth, *Geschichte Maria Theresia's*, 10 vols. (Vienna, 1863–1879). The indefatigable George P. Gooch has a volume on *Maria Thèresa and Other Studies* (New York, 1951). A new addition is Robert Pick's *Empress Maria Theresa: The Earlier Years, 1717–1757* (New York, 1966). This is the best documented and most detailed study in English on Maria Theresa's girlhood and the first seventeen years of her forty-year reign. On Joseph the most valuable older work is that by Paul von Mitrofanov, translated from

Russian to German as *Joseph II: Seine politische und kulturelle Tätigheit*, 2 vols. (Vienna, 1910). This may be supplemented by two later works, François Fejtö, *Un Habsbourg révolutionnaire, Joseph II* (Paris, 1953), and Fritz Valjavec, *Der Josephinismus: zur geistigen Entwicklung Österreichs im 18. und 19. Jahrhundert*, (Munich, 1945). Valjavec has subsequently broadened his researches to produce *Geschichte der abendländischen Aufklärung* (Vienna, 1961). In English there is an interesting biography by Saul Padover, *The Revolutionary Emperor: Joseph the Second, 1741–1790* (New York, 1934), and *Origins of Josephinism: Two Studies*, by Paul Peter Bernard (Colorado Springs, Col., 1962). Adam Wandruszka has written a good biography for Joseph's brother who succeeded him as emperor, *Leopold II*, 2 vols. (Vienna, 1963–1965).

CHARLES XII, GUSTAVUS III, AND STRUENSEE

For the history of Denmark, Norway, and Sweden in the eighteenth century, see B. J. Hovde, *The Scandinavian Countries, 1720–1865*, 2 vols. (Ithaca, N. Y., 1948); for Sweden alone, see Ingvar Andersson, *A History of Sweden* (London, 1956). The best biography of Charles XII is by Otto Haintz, *König Karl XII von Schweden*, 3 vols. (Berlin, 1958); a shorter work by Frans G. Bengtsson, *Charles XII* was published in Stockholm in 1960. The liveliest account of Gustavus III in English is still the account by Robert Nisbet Bain, *Gustavus III and His Contemporaries*, 2 vols. (London, 1894).

CHARLES III

François Rousseau, *Règne de Charles III d'Espagne*, 2 volumes (Paris, 1907) and Jean Sarrailh, *L'Espagne éclairée de la seconde moitié du XVIIIe siècle* (Paris, 1954) are good detailed accounts; in English there is a recent careful study by Richard Herr, *The Eighteenth Century Revolution in Spain* (Princeton, N. J. 1958). Harold Livermore's, *A History of Portugal* (Cambridge, England, 1947) provides a background for Pombal's activities, and Marcus Cheke has written a biography, *Dictator of Portugal: a Life of the Marquis of Pombal* (London, 1938).

CONTEMPORARY SOURCES

For passages from the writings of the seventeenth and eighteenth centuries, see Leo Weinstein, (ed.) *The Age of Reason: the Culture of the Seventeenth Century*, and Isidor Schneider, (ed.) *The Enlightenment: the Culture of the Eighteenth Century* (New York, 1965). Both have a broad selection, in English, with illustrations. *The Portable Age of Reason Reader*, edited by Crane Brinton, and *The Portable Voltaire*, edited by Ben Ray Redman, contain excellently chosen selections, and the same may be said for *French Philosophers from Descartes to Sartre*, edited by Leonard M. Marsak (Cleveland, 1961). Peter Gay has edited *John Locke on Education* (New York, 1964), and translated Voltaire's *Philosophical Dictionary*, 2 vols. (New York, 1962). Gay has also translated and edited Voltaire's *Candide*, which is available in many other editions. Montesquieu's *Persian Letters, Spirit of the Laws*, and *Considerations on the Causes of the Greatness of the Romans and Their Decline* are all available in English, the last named in a new translation by David Lowenthal (New York, 1965). Rousseau's *Social Contract* and *Emile* have appeared in various English editions. For Diderot and D'Alembert, N. Hoyt and T. Cassirer compiled and translated *Encyclopedia, Selections* (Indianapolis, Ind., 1965), and John Lough edited articles from the same source under the title *The Encyclopedia of Diderot and D'Alembert: Selected Articles* (London and New York, 1954), for which he provided an introduction but not a translation. Jay Luvaas has translated *Frederick the Great on the Art of War* (New York, 1966). William F. Reddaway edited *Documents of Catherine the Great: the Correspondence with Voltaire and the Instruction of 1767* (Cambridge, England, 1931). *The Memoirs of Catherine the Great*, translated by Moura Budberg and edited by Dominique Maroger (New York, 1964) is also available in paperback edition.

Index